Grenville A. J. (Grenville Arthur James) Cole

The Gypsy Road

A Journey From Krakow to Coblentz

Grenville A. J. (Grenville Arthur James) Cole

The Gypsy Road
A Journey From Krakow to Coblentz

ISBN/EAN: 9783744797153

Printed in Europe, USA, Canada, Australia, Japan

Cover: Foto ©Andreas Hilbeck / pixelio.de

More available books at **www.hansebooks.com**

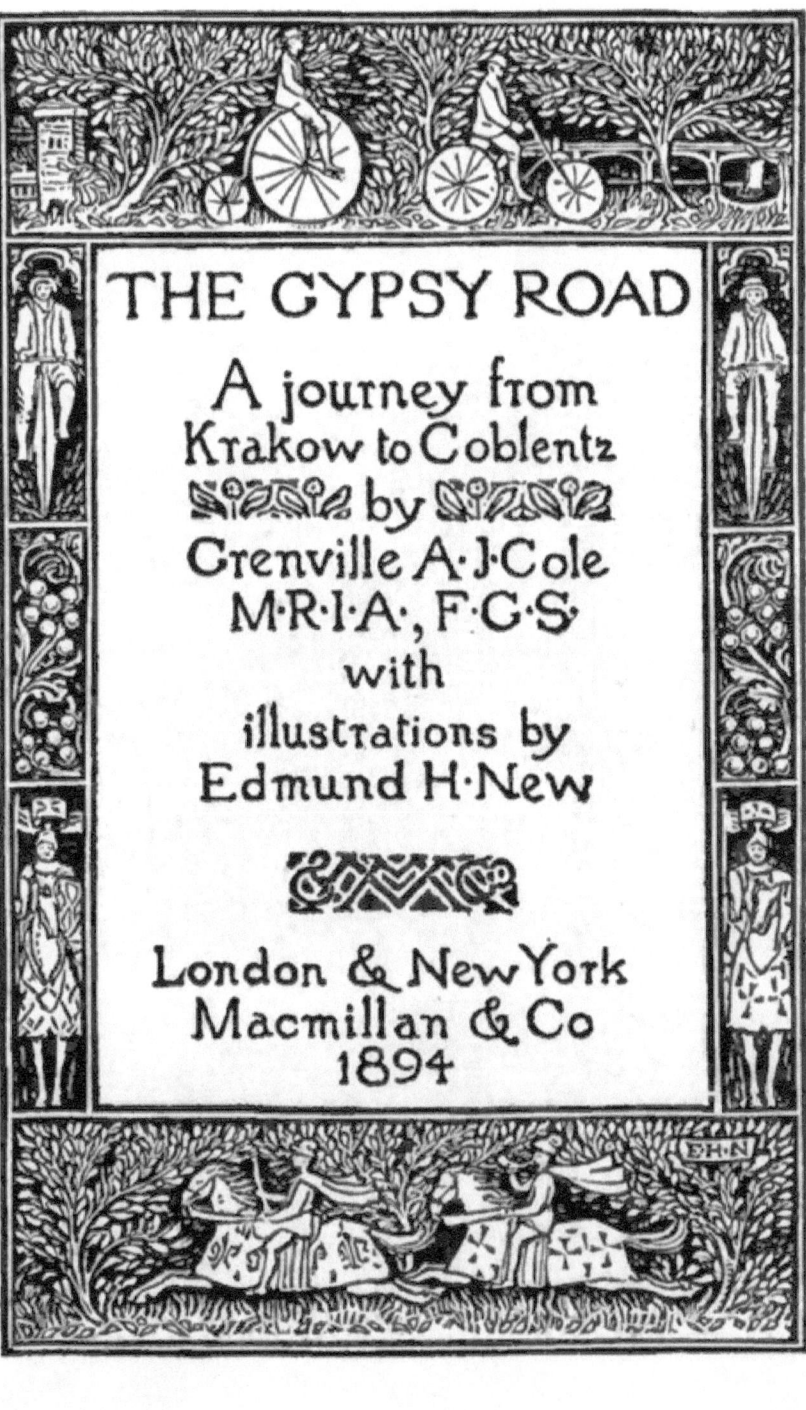

THE GYPSY ROAD

A journey from Krakow to Coblentz by Grenville A. J. Cole M.R.I.A., F.G.S. with illustrations by Edmund H. New

London & New York
Macmillan & Co
1894

DEDICATION

The Gypsies played;
And down the twilight avenue,
And all the leafy garden through,
The music wandered, like the air
Of God that rounds us everywhere
And is ourselves, unseen, unknown.

The Gypsies played;
And some who knew both east and west
Saw from the palace-quays of Pest
Their pleasure's fancy, France or Rome,
And some a sudden gleam of home,
Across their idle causerie.

The Gypsies played;
And some remembered how they heard
Such strains when Kossuth's armies stirred;
And some eyes filled with tears, and some
Smiled at the memories that come
Like petals from the roses blown.

        The Gypsies played;
And one who knew not any strain
Sat silent; yet he saw again
The long blue mountains and the plain
Stretch limitless; and straight he knew
His way across the world and through
All years to be; on him they bent
Their music, and he rose and went
Towards the dawn undoubtingly.

PREFACE

WHEN our grandfathers crossed Europe in a postchaise or a rumbling diligence, they did so with some show of gravity. Of late we have been so accustomed to step from the steamer to the sleeping-car, and from this to the day-express, that we have forgotten on the one hand the largeness, and on the other the detail of the earth. The rich variety of continental landscapes, the airy labours of the peasant, the growth or slumbering of towns, the interchange of ideas along the frontier, have become well-nigh lost to us in our rapid passages. But already a great change is coming over the methods of our travel, and the cyclist is exploring routes that have been closed for a good half-century. I have tried to describe in these pages the main features of such a journey.

Fortunately the countries dealt with—Poland, Hungary, the Slavonic ring—have a growing interest of their own, and offer a broad and attractive field to those who look eastward of the Rhine.

Mr. Gerard W. Butler, B.A., has kindly allowed me the use of his photographs, taken "upon tour," and I must thank Mr. New for having so accurately produced the illustrations from these and from a few rough sketches of my own.

G. A. J. C.

DUBLIN, *March* 1894.

TABLE TO ASSIST IN THE PRONUNCIATION OF PLACE-NAMES

Where no equivalent is given, the letter is not used in that language, or the pronunciation is practically as in German.

	Bohemian.	Polish.	Hungarian.
a	a in pan	a in pan	o in pot
á	a in father	...	a in father
c	ts	ts	ts
č	tch		
ć	...	tsj	
cs	...	...	tch
cz	...	tch	ts
d'	dy		
ě	ye		
é	a in babe	...	a in babe
í	ee in reed	...	ee in reed
ň	ny; Italian gn in campagna		
ń	...	Italian gn in campagna	
o	o in rod	o in rod	somewhat longer than o in rod
ó	o in rode	u in bull	o in rode
ö	...	...	longer than the German ö
ř	rsh		
s	as in English	as in English	sh

	Bohemian.	Polish.	Hungarian.
š	sh		
ś	...	sj	
sz	...	sh	s
t'	t'ye		
u	u in bull	u in bull	u in bull
ú	oo in food	...	oo in food
ů	oo in food, alters to o		
v	as in English	...	as in English
y	...	ui sounded close together; almost the South German ü	
ý	ee in reed		
z	as in English	as in English	as in English
ž	French j		
ź	...	zj	
ż	...	French j	

TABLE OF JOURNEYINGS

Through the shadow of the globe we sweep into the younger day;
Better fifty years of Europe than a cycle of Cathay.
                              TENNYSON. *Locksley Hall.*

		MILES.
GALICIA.	Betwixt Krakow and the Babagura	50
HUNGARY.	Betwixt the Babagura and the Morava	276
MORAVIA.	Betwixt the Morava and Iglau	96
BOHEMIA.	Betwixt Iglau and Schirnding	337
GERMAN EMPIRE.	Betwixt Schirnding and Coblenz	296
	TOTAL	1055

CONTENTS

	PAGE
I. Finis Poloniæ?	1
II. The Fort of Arva	17
III. Across the Szturecz	33
IV. Among the Silver-Mines	49
V. Against the Plains	67
VI. We Invade Moravia	83
VII. Untamed Bohemia	99
VIII. The Volcanic Zone	119
IX. The Heart of Europe	141
X. The Last Divide	153

FINIS POLONIÆ?

B

The kingdom of heaven is compared to a grain of mustard-seed, which is one of the least grains, but hath in it a property and spirit hastily to get up and spread. So are there states . . . that have but a small dimension of stem, and yet apt to be the foundation of great monarchies.
        BACON. *True Greatness of Kingdoms and Estates.*

THE town of Myslowitz has little to commend it, and its principal features can be studied without going farther than Warwickshire or Stafford. Dingy houses, a busy goods-yard, and a zone of smoking mine-chimneys, combine to impress the stranger with a sense of the disadvantages of commercial enterprise. Even the two red-brick spires, which rise somewhat superior to their surroundings, have lost half their colour in this gloomy air; and the absence of pointing between the bricks of the ordinary buildings gives them a look of hope deferred, as if they were waiting for better times. Various people had asked why we were going to Myslowitz. The fine policeman at Trzebinia, with his plumed

cap and fixed bayonet, had thought the circumstances suspicious; but at any rate we were not Russians. On the platform at Szczakowa a gentleman, probably an emissary of the Czar, addressed us in perfect English, and knew all about us in five minutes; but he also had his doubts as to our visiting Myslowitz for pleasure.

From above Myslowitz
The meeting of Russia, Prussia, & Austria, is behind the poplars.

We parted from him with the cordiality of diplomats, and the train carried him away into Russia before our eyes. And, indeed, why should we not go to Myslowitz?

The Prussians, on the other hand, were indifferent to our entry; perhaps, in our soft caps and knickerbockers, we were taken for commercial travellers in national costume. And yet it was sheer curiosity that had brought us on this summer's day to Myslowitz.

The high road rises slightly to the west, and a tall thin cross marks the summit of the ridge. Looking back over the cornfields, a strange panorama opens out, before which the fume of business may be well forgotten. In the hollow is an old farmstead, stretching out in a ruinous courtyard towards the fields; to its left, a chimney, rising from a mass of trees; to its right, a few tall poplars, between which one can see the green alluvial meadows of the Przemsza. Across the valley the dark woods rise steadily, leading up towards a plateau, the more distant waves of which are lost in a blue haze. The sun catches the hills yonder, and the smoke of two mines drifts along the far horizon. Men are working out there also, beyond the fringes of the woods.

Just behind those poplars, in the quiet meadows, is one of the critical points of Europe, beneath which, as we may say, the dynamite is laid, waiting only for some Guido Fawkes of policy to touch the fuse in Vienna, Petersburg, or Berlin. The three great empires meet there, with a display of particoloured posts; and, standing here in Prussian Silesia, we may realise the artificiality of modern frontiers, which are no longer lines of natural necessity, but of force. That narrow strip of meadow acts as a necromancer's circle, traced invisibly on the ground; the fiercest of spirits may hardly break it through. Turning from the Russian woodland, we look over into Austria on the right; and, as curious strangers, we may ask the people on either hand the name of their country and their race.

"We are Poles," they answer. Poland is a living name upon the frontier; you may call it West Galicia or what you will, but one country stretches for them from Warsaw to the far Karpathians. Freedom, it may be, on the one hand, centralised bondage on the other; will enthusiasm or despair be first to break the line?

Behind us a dash of rain comes from the dark Plessian forest; we look round from the meeting-point of nations, and over against us rises the great cross of Christ. In that sign kings have conquered, and their frontier-posts, for a token, are sprinkled with the blood of men.

We walked all day in Germany, and saw many pleasant sights in the hamlets of the forest-edge, ending with the magnificent avenue of old birch-trees that leads into Myslowitz from the south. But the sentiment of that European landscape remains with one as the train returns through the sand-hills and the patches of Scotch firs, till we alight again in Krakow, the centre of the happier life of Poland.

My companion was an Intellectual Observer—I know of no briefer title for his virtues—and we were merely waiting for the arrival of his bicycle to start for the Hungarian highlands. We paid daily visits to the serene goods-agent in the market-place, and were assured that these delays were part of the economy of nature. We noticed also that oil was always burning before a little shrine in the counting-house, as if to atone for the sins of omission of the railway companies; and each afternoon our hopes still rose with the flickering of that golden flame. Perhaps, however, it was extinguished nightly — a very Penelope among shrines.

Thus, at any rate, we came to know Krakow better. I had ridden from Zólyom over the Szturecz with another English friend; and we had alighted finally by rail in Poland, the nickel of our machines gleaming with a certain incongruity in the station-lamplight under notice-boards marked *Wchod* and *Wychód*. Then followed a week of visions rather than of sight-seeings, such as one must go to Krakow to appreciate. In two days, however, we had settled down, and received the Observer with the dignified air of men familiar with the East. For his part, he displayed no such triviality as emotion; the impressions he receives are not at once made public, and perhaps some side-light

A plain red Church in Krakow. (from our bedroom)

thrown on them long after alone reveals their depth.

Professor Jandaurek has compared Krakow with Venice; others must have thought of Nürnberg. But such suggestions convey very little meaning; for, just as Tyrol has Innsbruck, and France has Bourges, and England her Warwick and Ludlow, so Poland has her Krakow, something to be seen and understood if one would turn at all the forgotten leaves of history.

The Florian gate and outwork Krakow.

Though one may now walk in from all sides across the fine ring of gardens, it is still well to enter the city by the Florian Gate, protected by its bold red outwork, and to see the peasants lifting their caps before the shrine that lights this Gothic archway. The narrow street leads quickly to the square in which the business of Krakow centres; but the pleasant shop-fronts and fine old market-house are not the first attractions. We turn instinctively to St. Mary's, push open the door, and it is as if a veil were lifted—the curtain rises on the East.

Outwardly, there is something richly fantastic in the two red-brick towers, differing in design, and set with pilasters and pinnacles of bronze; but the glory of this building is within. From floor to roof is an amazing glow of colour, every inch of surface gilt or painted, blue, crimson, terracotta, or warm brown. Altars, brightly decked, and adorned with carvings or bronzework at every point, line the aisles, and culminate in Veit Stoss's huge panelled altarpiece under the tall east windows. Peasants are on their knees on the stone floor, which they kiss as part of their devotions—rough red-bearded carters, in their high boots and long white tunics, confined at the waist by ornamented leather belts; and women, perhaps barefooted, with wide blue aprons, and with white kerchiefs on their heads. One must indeed come east for such a scene, with which the vaults and ribs of gold and vermilion far overhead, and the huge crucifix, seeming almost to float above the choir, are in the fullest, richest harmony.

The builders of the Alhambra were equally daring in their use of colour; but our Western notions as to what is fitting in a cathedral have long inclined towards the barest grey of nature. Moreover, in our latest reformations, we have too often stripped away the plaster, instead of using it to bring back warmth and colour. The huge frescoed surfaces in St. Barbara's at Kutna Hora in Bohemia, and the remains of colouring in the chapel of St. Wenceslaus in Prag, show that the restorers of St. Mary's have merely revived the spirit of the fourteenth-century founders.

Outside again in the sunlight, one realises the possibilities of red brick, as one realises them in Dublin daily, and as our forefathers may have done in London before fogs and noonday darkness were invented. At Hampton Court also, when the sun is low across the gleaming reaches of the river, one may forget the house-boats, and the steamer up from the great city, and feel something of the air of Krakow, something very strange and far away.

The Observer at length received his bicycle, the graceful old "ordinary" to which enthusiasts still cling; and the day of our departure came. My tricycle was wheeled out of the great stable of the *Hôtel Poller;* our hands were kissed by the fine young "Boots"—again a touch of Poland—and we rattled over the *pavé* and across the little fruit-market to the post-office.

Here I was at once arrested by an officer of police, who addressed me courteously in Polish; he had taken us for visitors from Warsaw, to be closely scanned accordingly. Had we not seen in the newspapers how an unhappy disseminator of "socialistic" literature had just received three weeks' imprisonment, and how the "young Poles" on both sides of the frontier were freely exciting the imagination? Truly, you cannot divide a people by drawing lines upon a map; and this little city of Krakow has its memories. Many of these bearded men around us were born into the free republic, and can recall the first planting of the yellow flag on the fort at Kosciuszko's Hill, and the quartering of Austrian soldiers in the courts of Kasimierz the Great. United Poland is a dream; but the hearts of our grandchildren may yet glow at the name of Krakow, when Venice and Strassburg have settled down in middle-class contentment.

The crowd that quickly gathers round such strange objects as touring cyclists began slowly to disperse; we were speaking mere German; our ignorance of national affairs was easily discerned. The officer bade us good speed, and we moved on towards the Vistula. It was a Sunday, and the Jews were active everywhere, after their peaceful Sabbath; not to be outdone, the Christian shopkeepers were also in full swing, holding their own, indeed, only by the seventh day's labour. In Krakow one man in four is an Israelite, and the long dark coat is to be seen on all sides. These Jews are a thin, keen-eyed, unathletic race; and, indeed, how should a boy learn to run when encumbered with the traditional gaberdine? The gaberdine may vary from a heavy ulster, girt at the waist, to something like a lady's waterproof, and is not to be commended for picturesqueness. Let us hope, however, that no one nowadays imitates the conduct of Antonio.

From the busy suburb of Podgórze, picturesque with booths, and stalls, and peasantry in full costume, we struck the open highway, and the tour began.

Cromwell Road, S. Kensington, or the High Street of Kingston, even in their palmiest days, could scarcely vie in irregularity with the way to Mogilany; but we knew that Hungary had better things in store. This day, indeed, was our only ride in Poland; but we saw enough to interest us. The little log-houses, with detached barns, look neat enough outwardly, and give an air of peasant-proprietorship as they lie scattered among the hills. We had left the military railways behind us, and plunged into a primitive agricultural country; in the midst of this is Myślenice, where we halted—a large village of low houses, mostly one-storied, among which we failed to recognise the "*auberge fort belle*" in which the energetic mineralogist Beudant found consolation in 1818.

Thence we had a pretty riverside road to Lubień, where the church drew us aside a while; yet in this country it is only one of many. It is completely wooden, with two vermilion pear-shaped towers, culminating in silver bulbs, which bear tall crosses. The smaller tower—or spire, or, scientifically speaking, spherospire—rises from the centre of the roof, and the whole effect is romantically oriental. The postmaster and his family gathered round us, in the friendly manner of the country, and drank good speed to us as we left for the uplands in the dusk. It is a fine climb over the first foot-hills of the Karpathians, amid the welcome smell of pine-forests, and down again to the great valley of the Skawa. In the grey light we could see the massive ridges on the Hungarian frontier, and perhaps even the giant Tátra, cloud-capped in the darkening south.

It was a stirring run down on Skomielna, where the lights of the little inn seemed to call us at the cross-roads; but we were bound a stage farther yet. At Zabornia, however, on the last descent to the river, we had some difficulty in distinguishing our house in simple starlight; but Herr Wallner, a characteristic Jewish host, came to his door and received us warmly. The inn is a typical one-storied wooden building, picturesque in its roof and its veranda; but its owner speaks sadly and admiringly of the commonplace modern hotels that accompany the railway down below. This railway, moreover, has drawn off the old traffic from the Krakow road. We have heard this kind of complaint in England, and cycling is its obvious remedy.

Our companion at Wallner's was a commercial traveller in agricultural machines, who knew the Austrian empire fairly—to know a tenth part of it is a liberal education. Bosnia, he said, would no doubt suit us; but it was bad for business. Truly, swords are more prized than ploughshares on the frontier. We had to produce Bradshaw's map of Europe to show the position of our far-off islands; but our friend knew well the power of England. "You have," said he, "a fortress on the Bosporus, to keep the Russians out of the Mediterranean."

As usual, the little parlour was the common dormitory; and, when our meal was cleared away, we noticed how the Commercial, with graceful modesty, chose the couch rather than either of the beds. These beds were clean, with home-made linen, and we turned in gladly; but at a later period our friend's discretion was explained. The characteristic inhabitants of Poland, those insidious enemies that leap upon you even in the leafy gardens of Krakow, dwell in undisturbed happiness at Zabornia. People have resented the frequent references to them in the sparkling pages of Miss Dowie—why should we call her by a new name?—but really they form so much of the life of Poland that truth cannot pass them over. Suffice it that the foe can be avoided by crossing the frontier into Hungary.

THE FORT OF ARVA

c

The battled towers, the donjon keep,
The loophole grates, where captives weep,
The flanking walls that round it sweep,
   In yellow lustre shone.
The warriors on the turrets high,
Moving athwart the evening sky,
   Seem'd forms of giant height:
Their armour, as it caught the rays,
Flash'd back again the western blaze,
   In lines of dazzling light.

                      SCOTT. *Marmion.*

ABOUT 5 a.m. we began the day, and our host walked in and out of the common-room with his pipe as we were dressing, while the servant mingled washing materials and breakfast in the primitive manner of the East. There was to be a market down at the Baths of Rabka, and the Intellectual Observer went there to study the costumes. He made, later on, some remarkable water-colour drawings, not to say paintings, as a preliminary to his large picture of " The Market of Rabka," which reminds those who have not seen it of Fortuny, with touches of De Blaas.

The road south, however, was also full of brilliant bands of peasantry, and we had a sort of fancy fair all through the morning. Most people rode to market in the long country cart, here usually drawn by horses. The body is a great elastic pine-stem, roughly squared, with a pair of small wheels at either end. The sides of the cart are ladder-like, as is so often seen in the hay-carts of central Europe; and they are easily detachable. You sit on the pole, with your legs thrust through an interstice of the side-ladder, and your feet resting on a smaller pole slung outside between the pairs of wheels. Eight or nine bright bare-footed girls, in blue or red skirts, full white sleeves, and the gayest of kerchiefs on their heads, driven by the important male of the party, in his white wool garments and dark broad-brimmed hat, form a picture of natural mirth, the memory of which abides with one for months in our sober western isles. The horses were naturally shy of cycles, especially of the high one, and our progress was slow upon this crowded highway. One old lady and her husband were carried away into a cornfield and incontinently overturned; but, like peasants in general, they seemed rather pleased than otherwise, especially when we helped to pick up the pieces, and to tie the cart together again. When the Observer finally insisted on atoning with a gulden, these worthy people doubtless felt that they had done a good day's work.

Another party, a youthful one of some seven

or eight persons, rushed down a bank, careered over the stubble, and finally drove fearlessly up again, the girls laughing heartily at the adventure, which would certainly have been the ruin of a shorter and more rigid vehicle.

Soon after mid-day we saluted the Hungarian frontier-post on the divide of Babagura, among broad grassy slopes and patches of pink moorland flowers. At once the road improved, the villages became neater; and Tandlich's inn at Orávka was at least worthy of Bohemia. The two young men who attended on us in the combined bedroom and parlour were, indeed, forerunners of the gentlemen-innkeepers whom we were to meet later in the tour. Military service had done something for them; but nationality was their kindest teacher.

After a time we rose to an open moorland, covered with alluvial gravels, with clear little streams descending from the forest; and here we bathed, dragging the machines over the rough cow-pasture to the plashing bends of the Jolossna, and guided by the copious advice and goodwill of a wagon-load of travellers on the highway. One Jewish gentleman overflowed in friendliness. Stay—before we went to the river, would the Observer be so good as to mount upon his machine? It would be such an act of kindness—the rural postman, who was of the party, had never seen a high bicycle—it was an opportunity. There! The hero sprang into the saddle and rode successfully across the rough timbers of the bridge. Farewell, kindly wayfarers, Jews and Poles and Slovaks! These meetings also are unknown to travellers by rail.

Later, a strange melancholy settled in the air. The near slopes of the broad moor grew dark, the farther hills became pallid, and finally blotted out in rain. It was one of those beautiful soft landscapes, with rich touches of brown and black and purple, that carry one back to Western Ireland, or to the floor of Assynt and Arisaig; and one forgets the Karpathian barrier, pale and ghostly in the south, and begins almost to look ahead for the first white gleaming of the sea.

We were across this foot-hill also, and down against the waters of the Arva, through euphonious Trzstena, and on between the banks to Turdossin. The *Black Eagle* in this town is one of the good old hostels, the true European caravanserai, with all the rooms upon one floor, opening on the court, which is the garden; and the stable is not under you, as in many parts of Germany and Switzerland, but commodiously on a level, its huge doors facing on the highway.

As we strolled about in the yellow light of sunset, we saw how the pine-log houses, built upon a white concrete base, were little removed from those in pictures of Siberia. There is a careless free-and-open luxury, moreover, about the width of the suburban streets, which are much less conventional than those of the business quarter. In this, Turdossin resembled Zólyom, where my wheels had first alighted from the railway into the fascination of a Hungarian village. Zólyom, indeed, had proved a magnificent introduction. To leave the cushions of the express, and to ride straightway up the cart-grooved expanse that is here regarded as a street, under a great feudal castle, and among ox-wagons and two-horsed carts moving gaily in all directions—this gives the mind the sort of thrill that we knew as schoolboys, when we dived abruptly from Milk Street and Cheapside into the wilds of *Ivanhoe* or *The Talisman*. And there was a market that day in Zólyom, with yellow-faced Mongolian-looking men, their long straight hair drawn to the front and falling in two plaits towards the waist; and robust bare-armed sunburnt women, in pink and blue, white and yellow; and clamorous half-naked gypsies, with bronze-black skins, unkempt, unwashed, and absolutely savage. Well, we were back in

Hungary now; and the East has always something new in store.

The *Black Eagle* of Turdossin gave us dinner, bed, and breakfast for the sum of 2s. 10d. each, a bill characteristic of the country. From its sheltering wings we continued to descend the Arva, between cliffs, and châlet villages, and steep wooded cones, eager for the great sight that had been promised us by every one on the road. At last, at a bend of the river, the huge crag rose, with the fortress of Arva pile upon pile on the arête—Arvaváralja, they call the village, a name for poets and for kings.

It serves no purpose to say that this is the finest castle in Europe, for nobody has seen them all, and castles are as incomparable as cathedrals. Richmond on the Swale may rival Kronburg on the Inn; but the beauty of each is interwoven with its landscape as a whole. And to enjoy such a scene to fulness, one must see visions and dream dreams—one should have the retrospective second sight that became an art in *Peter Ibbetson*. Here, "under the fort of Arva," we can at least picture the pageantry of the Anjou kings, with Louis the Great riding north to Poland, the narrow track filled with jostling men-at-arms, their steel caps slung behind them in the hot sunlight; and we can see them halting at mid-day by the stream, or pouring into the wine-shops of Turdossin with all the frank self-confidence of men who have never known defeat. They had humiliated Naples and Venice, the Wallachians, Turks, and Germans, and now Poland came to them as a comfortable bequest; but it was like being presented with a den of lions. The Krakow road proved not an easy one to travel.

Yet common ills are the final healers of old feuds. Thus we find Poles in Hunyadi's army of the Balkans, keeping back the strenuous Turk; and again, after four wild centuries, Galician recruits in revolt against Austria in 1849; they are Poles, they say, and have no quarrel with the Magyars. And did not Bem, a Pole, though his name at first got vaguely into English newspapers as "Böhm," head the defence of Vienna in '48 as an act of international courtesy, and then reappear in a more definite manner as the champion of Hungarian independence? Poles and Magyars, brethren in arms, had a way of extorting admiration; and the old fort of Arva looked down on them as they drove even the Russians north in the fierce July of '49. Arvaváralja knows better than most of us that the peasants make history, not the kings. The men who fell in silence at

Borodino, the *chouans* of Vendée, the *sansculottes* of Paris, the brown-coats of New Ross and Arklow, the New Model and the Ironsides—these are, for the most part, vague and shadowy masses; but when these masses combine for a new purpose, when they meet to bury the last breechloader, then there will be no more use or place for kings.

There was ample time for contemplation in the fine hotel at Arvaváralja, for the rain descended for five hours. Among other worthies, we came across an Italian foreman engaged upon a mountain-road. These Italian engineers have become almost nomads, a revival of the old masonic guilds; one year we found them cooking their soup beside a railway in the Baden hills; in another they were building the forts on the St. Gotthard, which are designed to cut off Italy from her German allies.

The fort of Arva, with a whole village and a church in it, climbing the arête from the boulders of the rapid river, gave us plenty to look at from our windows; on the very summit of the crag, and sheer above us, a pale yellowish tower, roofed in and perfect as the rest, grew from the rock itself in the purest fantasy and defiance.

In a somewhat treacherous whiteness of the

A Tower of Arva-Vátalja

air we descended the rugged valley to Alsó Kubin—to quote its official name, the true one varying as usual with the language that is spoken locally. Its own Slovak people call it Dolnj Kubin—Lower Kubin, anyway. The German place-names commonly appear upon our maps, and are used when one is speaking German; but I have tried to adopt the national ones in these pages, since they alone are seen upon the sign-posts; and there is no more reason for translating them into German than into French. The latter process would, at any rate, be more palatable to the Magyars. The Slovak names, however, will vanish from the Karpathians more slowly than the German ones, for they are the real article, and the Magyar forms are dictated from the Government at Budapest. Thus Kecskés has been painted up in the village of Kozelnik, and Zsarnócza in Zarnovice; but people still call them "the new names." The Hungarian and Slavonic languages can no longer be ignored; the very cumbrousness of German has brought them to the front again, and all our maps and geography-books are already out of date.

At Alsó Kubin one final highland alone divided us from the Alps of Liptó. On this open moor we passed and repassed two old merchants driving in a great country cart or carriage, just as the observant Dr. Bright did some eighty years ago. But these men knew their business, and maintained antique and independent ways; for they had four or five horses running freely beside them, ready to take their turn in the traces. The sheep of the great Hungarian plain have also preserved patriarchal customs; when driven from one village to another, they spread out like a flood on either side of the unfenced roadway, and the white-skirted and blue-aproned shepherd keeps the broad mass moving, with its curved front advancing slowly, like the Armada in Plymouth Sound.

Suddenly we passed from moors to mountains, and were under the pale walls of limestone, and amid the spray of torrents roaring through the Tátra spurs. In the midst of this wild contrast lay the perched village of Dubova-Valaska, with a desperately sheer drop out of it. At the mouth of the gorge we swung out into the open pastoral country, while on our left the pallid ruin of Likavka rose, like a vision of old feuds, against the rain-swept forest and the clouds that came and went beneath the crags. For five hundred years at least it held the valley—a vast mansion as much as a castle—until Rakóczy, the

Cromwell of 1700, shattered this Basing House and left it to tell its own tale to the Magyars.

And so down to the Vág, here innocent enough among the meadows, and into busy Rózsahegy, "the Rose Hill," where every slope, notwithstanding, is dark with mountain-pines.

At the *Hôtel Kralicka* we were greeted as if we had returned from the Polish wars; for I had stopped two nights here when going north. Even a Professor from the capital, who was photographing in the High Tátra, told us of the two cycling Englishmen who had arrived a week before. And after dinner there was the customary visitation of the machines by curious townsmen, a solemn scene, with candles in our hands, which dimly lighted the great upstairs room in which they lay, with its massive tables, and its dust, and the old minstrels' gallery at one end.

ACROSS THE SZTURECZ

D

> The splendour falls on castle walls
>   And snowy summits old in story:
> The long light shakes across the lakes,
>   And the wild cataract leaps in glory.
> Blow, bugle, blow, set the wild echoes flying,
> Blow, bugle; answer, echoes, dying, dying, dying.
>
>   TENNYSON. *The Princess.*

AND now for the true highlands, that stand between the grey north and the vast red-gold of the cornfields, between Poland and the Danube plain. In the forest-clad Karpathians, which do not even reach up to the snow-line, the geologist can pick out the essential features of the Alps, of which, indeed, they form the north-eastern prolongation. The schists and gneiss and granite of the core occasionally crop out at the surface; the axis is the same as in Switzerland, but has been kept at a lower level and out of the way of denudation. From Rózsahegy to the valley of the Garam we pass from one set of Tertiary foot-hills to another, and cross the grey Secondary limestones, folded over and even surmounting the gneissose mountain-ridge. If the great European earth-

movements are still in progress, we see here the birth of the Hungarian Alps, the main mass of which is still below the level of the sea. The opening of the movements was marked, as usual, by brilliant volcanic action, and the relics of these cones and lava-flows were the chief attraction of our present journey to the south.

It is not so far from one railway to the other, some thirty-four miles of mountain; but in the journey the modern traveller will realise the delights of the old Swiss passes, before *Hôtels d'Angleterre* arose among the châlets and cantonal costumes were banished. On the Szturecz I lorded it over the Observer, after the manner of experienced travellers, having actually crossed the pass before; and, if the scenery bears repetition, the road does also, for it is one of the best in Hungary. The Observer, however, has a higher opinion of eastern engineers than I have, for his bicycle, in the worst of circumstances, generally found a foot-track at the side. In nine years I have had so little to complain of in the tricycle as a touring medium—*une voiture*, as they say in France—that I will frankly admit that in Hungary and Bohemia the bicycle has the fairer chances. This is mainly due to the lavish use of unrolled road-metal; but on the Szturecz route dusty groovings were the enemies. Even the Observer dismounted unexpectedly in one of these; and the fact is worthy of mention. It was the only mishap of the kind in a thousand miles of touring. A race of bicyclists is rising, often "backed like a weasel," and ignorant alike of the beauties of the "good old ordinary," and of the ease of propulsion of the tricycle. For such these pages will have only a melancholy interest; it may console them if I add that a "safety," constructed for human and not simian use, is, after all, the ideal machine for Austria-Hungary.

The valley is gentle up to Oszada, and one meets regular tourists descending in carriages from the baths of Korinica, which are hidden away here among the Alpine spurs. But the drivers of these Excellencies still wear local costumes; the "English groom," the ambition of Europe, has not yet penetrated hither; and even the Excellencies themselves are cordial to the cyclist. The peasant-women, however, from Krakow onwards, give one the truest and unfailing greeting. We have heard it in Polish and Slovakish, and I am ashamed to say I cannot quote the phrase; but it ends with the great word of brotherhood, Christus, and the good priest of Krivá, who blessed us yesterday as we passed, cannot give it a finer meaning than these simple toilers of the fields.

It is a grand thing to see a woman of these highlands come along the road into the village, her coloured apron folded up towards the waist, close-kirtled, leaving her free to stride forward like a man, the short white woollen skirt swaying

Peasant woman returning from the hayfield
Revuca
Hungary

as she moves, her arms swinging, and probably a rake in her right hand and a bundle on her back, fastened by bands across the chest. Upright, stalwart, energetic, she is the true mother of the hill-men; sometimes she walks barefoot, her legs coloured the grand copper-bronze of her bare arms; but for longer distances she wears high boots like the men, or the twisted leather bands that are used so often in the Slovak districts.

The people above Rózsahegy are mostly a fair-haired race, the women clothing themselves in white, with red and yellow embroidery on the shoulder-bands and sleeveless bodices, in contrast to the rich blues and pinks that are common in the Magyar plain. Some of the men wear veritable corselets of stiff leather, ornamented with incised and painted lines, which seem relics of the days of armour. These singular waistcoats, as we may regard them nowadays, are loosely fitting, the neck coming through one round hole, and the arms through wide ones in the sides. Everywhere we may notice how the coat is an appendage, slung at the back as in the Hussars, and only to be worn in heavy rain. The real outer garment is the black sleeveless vest, highly embroidered, the white sleeves of the shirt, close-fitting or bell-shaped, coming out from under it with a pretty contrast. The Slovak also wears a very wide felt hat, turned up all round at the brim, and flat in the crown; and he embroiders green knots on the front of his white wool trousers, down the thighs. The richness of his red and green embroidery on Sundays is worthy of an ancient missal. The interlacing knots and lines may have descended from old customs of body-painting, and even of tattooing; but it would be unkind to press the analogy with the savage, when the results, even in the nineteenth century, add so greatly to the gaiety of nations.

These fine, tall, clean-shaven men are apt to enjoy their Sunday in the wine-and-beer shop (*bor és sör* is a phrase that becomes ingrained in us); and they will sing songs there with a sentimental dreariness worthy of the English labourer. And when at length they turn out in the evening, they go unsteadily tramping up the valley, the black-blue sky ablaze with stars above them, and the streamlets making a far ripple of music through the pines, and a soft air blowing from the colder crests of the divide. Are they taught, indeed, as in sterner England, to despise this world around them, and so come to conclude with Faustus,

> An this be hell, I'll willingly be damn'd here?

The Observer found much to photograph in the pretty little wooden village of Oszada, and friendly inhabitants came out who had seen the two cyclists pass ten days before. It is gratifying to one's vanity to be remembered, especially by pleasant country gentlemen and their daughters; things are different on the Ripley Road—for many reasons.

The long string of hamlets now called Három Revuca, "the Three Revucas," gives one every chance of seeing the peasant, and particularly his children. The latter are fair-haired little creatures, the boys in big hats and loose white shirts and trousers, ending

Három Revuca
Hungary

well above the ankle; the girls dress mainly in white also, with short bell-like sleeves and coloured aprons. The apron plays a great part everywhere in Austria-Hungary—greater even among the men than among the women.

To-day every house, whether plain pine or whitewashed, was gleaming in the sunlight, and the smooth grey shingle roofs simply shone like the lead of an old château. All were, of course, one-storied, and sometimes a shrine, in a little detached tower of its own, guarded the recessed doorway. Wood is usually stacked against the wall under the eaves, and the children and old people sit upon it. A log is often thus saved from dissection, and remains as a convenient seat for the family and its visitors. Every facility is given for intercourse—for gossip, if you will; I doubt if there is even a lock on the front door. These sociable little hamlets look very sweet when compared with the Venetian-blind and bell-pull civilisation of artisan life, say in Battersea and Sheffield.

There were gypsies also, bronze by race and black by custom, living a savage life in wooden huts, which are often placed against some sheltering rock. Begging is absolutely habitual with them when strangers are in sight, and the children's mouths open and shut mechanically over the word *krajczár* or *kreuzer*. They will come running from long distances across the grassy slopes, like the wild animals that they are, reminding one of collies scenting a stranger in the Highlands. Their clothes are just what come to hand, boys and girls exchanging casually, and the colour becoming subdued by usage, until it is finally the same dull black as themselves. Clothes are, indeed, clearly an encumbrance, as every child of nature feels. The gypsy boy favours an old shirt, completely open down the front; and I have seen a lithe brown girl of twelve, running more gracefully than a deer, and content with a long black sleeveless jacket, embroidered in the national red and green.

Mrs. Pennell, in her beautiful essays on the gypsies, minimises their inartistic savagery; perhaps in the great plain, where water is scarcer, they may have more appreciation of it. In the northern uplands their squalor is neither passionate nor picturesque; we feel ourselves transported suddenly to the Congo, or the Australian bush, and we almost tremble to see the spotless Slovak children playing in the same roads and sitting on the same fence-rails as these veritable imps of darkness.

The highest Revuca hamlet is passed, and the valley narrows abruptly to a mere corridor of limestone; beyond it is the true mountain-pass, with the torrent and the steep pine-glades, and the road climbing in huge curves a thousand feet higher to the ridge. The thoughtful cyclist pushes his machine; at every corner we look down upon the thick-set spikes of fir-trees, and catch some glimpse of the white roadway winding like a serpent in the ravine. The Szturecz is scarcely a pass; it is a climb up the head of one *cul-de-sac* and down the steep face of another, so that one seems called on suddenly to cross the mountain-wall where no natural notch appears. At the summit, 1069 mètres above the sea, which is, after all, child's-play to the Arlberg or the St. Gotthard, a characteristically novel and Karpathian landscape opens out. The forms of the hills are sharp enough, but the forest in reality clothes every ridge and crest. The black serrations of the pines run up and down the outlines where one expects to find sheer crags; only here and there some grey scar shows among the trees, with perhaps a long groove under it, where the boulders in winter have cut their channel through the woods. If we compare this style of forest with that of Fontainebleau or Compiègne, we at once require a new name for it; it is like comparing sea-cliffs with the sea.

The Tátra crags behind us loomed up clear and grey, the hot rocks pallid in the sunlight; then came the great plunge into the forest, and we did not see Northern Europe again till we got into the mazed perplexity of German states at Coburg.

The descent is more serpentinous than the

ascent, but the trees mask its wildness, until at last there is a piece so straight and steep that the stones refuse to stay in their places; and here we both walked, like good old stagers. Delicious interludes of wooden hamlets and green meadows in the clearings brought us to Ó hegy or Altgebirg (the Old Hill), the centre of the valley, where a famous pilgrimage-chapel stands. The young men at the inn were ready with a welcome.

"You are back again so soon from Poland? And what has become of the other gentleman?"

I said he had returned to his business in England.

"To England? Think of it!"

One might as well have said Kerguelen Island.

They call out to us down the road, "There now, a pleasant journey! And come and see Altgebirg again!"

Dust and ruts and woodlands form the entry to Besterczebánya (Neusohl). *Bánya* indicates a mine, copper prevailing in this instance, and Saxon miners were invited hither as early as the thirteenth century. Their sturdy persons were probably wanted by King Béla as much as their scientific skill; for Batu Khan and his Mongols had just cleared out the country, pouring over the Karpathians with a gay disregard for average humanity and with the aimlessness of the plains of Asia. The repetition of such an invasion is always possible in Europe; it forms, indeed, the great unfulfilled prophecy of Rousseau—first Russia, then the Tartars. "*Tous les rois de l'Europe travaillent de concert à l'accélérer.*"

Some one had chalked *Vivant Vacationes* on the school-door, a cheerful greeting as we rode into Besterczebánya. The main street is ancient, with prehistoric paving-stones, as knobby as those of some Cheshire towns, which shall be nameless. The best view of the place is gained, however, from the suburb on the Garam, where one looks up at the castle-platform and the pair of towers, tall and bulbous, with the dark mass of the Karpathians as a background. The story of these towns is terribly alike; the dash of horsemen to the gates, the sweep of fire up the narrow street, the flight to the castle-platform, the spearmen picking off the little children as they run; then the siege, the church-roofs blazing, hot water and pitch streaming on the assailants from the towers; and finally a parley with the survivors, a sprinkling of good faith and a bucketful of bad, and a general gathering together of the pieces, the carpenters and builders profiting by the whole concern. The women suffered largely, as was just and natural; the men felt that they had seen a bit of life; and the professional men-at-arms went swaggering off on a new foray. Whoever raised a standard or crushed a rebellion, the towns were sure to pay for it; and between

Inn at Hajnik

breakfast and dinner they often ran the course of a civil war.

Then, along the nations' meeting-line, one never knew who was to be master. The worthy burghers might be carried off as hostages by the Bohemians, might be rescued by the robber-princes of the Vág, and finally be decapitated by their lawful sovereign for neglect of their official duties. I fancy they would have declared in favour of anybody, if only he had left his card genteelly, instead of flaring up the high street like an unpremeditated meteor.

This evening we were bound farther, under the cloudless gold of sunset, with the young moon pale in the west above the low volcanic hills. The vast fields were silent, and we pushed across one of them to the wooded bank of the Garam. It was delicious, after the last brisk nine miles, to lie full length in the cool rushing water, the stones sliding away from under one with the force of it, and nothing visible but trees and sky, as the twilight was deepening into night. The labourers were home already; only a few birds, glad to linger, were calling softly from the fields.

We climbed up the bank again in time to reach the spires of Hajnik in the dusk, and were received at the archways of Kupcsek József's inn. In Hungary, by the bye, the Christian name, being less important, waits upon the surname—Kossuth Lájos, Louis Kossuth.

AMONG THE SILVER-MINES

E

Glück auf!

OUR room was characteristic —a bed at each side, the table for meals in the middle, and the mountain-air blowing across from one open window to the other. At 5.30 a.m. the bare-footed girl, always with her white kerchief on her head, walks in for our shoes, and continues to come in and out, while we answer her grave salutations from beneath the crimson quilts. Soon we are up and breakfasting, while Kupcsek, in white shirt and trousers, helps the girl to tidy up the room around us.

It was now hot almost with the hotness of the plain; one could picture the Danube gleaming white under the pallid rocks of Buda, and the vast cornland stretching south and east in waves of burnished bronze. To our left the castle of Zólyom quivered against the dark band of the pines; and on all sides the air was full of the grand odour of hot woodlands.

It is a well-graded climb to the mining country, and the dry slopes show everywhere huge volcanic bombs, pink and crumbling, in a matrix of absorbent dust, the deposits of the eruptions that accompanied the Karpathian fold. The watercourses were dead and dry, or marked by mere iron-brown filmy tricklings between the banks of yellow ash. Kecskés is the last agricultural hamlet, poor indeed, the roofs of the rough log-houses covered with turf, brown, ragged, and often moss-grown; but in a dry land even poverty seems happy and picturesque. There is no mud, no grime—unless you are a gypsy; no dirt sinks in and clings; even fifty inches of rain, crowded into one definite season, at least leave you cheerful for the other.

Above Kecskés, round the head of the combe, the furnaces of Bélabánya (Dilln) bring one at once to business. Red-brick sheds, roads black with ashes, rusty cog-wheels cast aside, and children of uncertain complexion, are here, as usual, the accompaniments of industry. A machicolated white church-tower, nobly bulbous, dominates the crowded bank of houses. Where, however, is the great town of Selmeczbánya?

Selmeczbánya or Schemnitz is probably the

most famous mining centre of Austria-Hungary. There is a quaint tradition that, somewhere in the eighth century, the first mineralogical students appeared upon the highland, in the form of two snakes, one of whom had collected gold-dust and the other silver-dust upon its scales. A herdsman

A hillside in Bélábanya

named Sebnicz perceived them, and doubtless cautioned them in the customary manner. Without pioneers, the man of business would be nowhere; the simple-minded snakes were skinned, and Sebnicz founded Selmeczbánya.

The volcanic rocks, rhyolites, andesites, and basalts, associated with all this mineral richness, had, as has been already hinted, formed the object of our present tour; but when one sees the tangle of oak and fir, and combe and mountain, and the white church-towers peeping from the woods, one does not seem to need much excuse for climbing hither from the Garam.

Selmeczbánya lies well hidden away in the

High Street Selmeczbánya

next steep hollow after Bélabánya. Above it and west of it is a high divide, across which one has constantly to climb, a grand narrow ridge, fir-covered, where one may walk for miles amid majestic sunset—or, if you will, sunrise—views. On dropping over from Bélabánya one perceives a house or two, then a gateway dated 1588, a paved street, and a breakneck descent past the huge brown School of Mines; but only at the foot of this does the town reveal itself, stretching high up a narrow groove to the right, like a sunnier nobler Halifax, with its tall towers

Market Place
Selmeczbánya
Hungary

around the most oblique of market-places, until finally there is room only for one stream and a foot-track to the black fir-trees of the divide.

One pushes; one shoves; one labours upward to the simple old *Szálloda a Szőlőhoz*, which is briefly translatable as *The Grapes*. Every arrival, by road or rail, does this, and the singular position of Selmeczbánya is duly impressed both on the commercial and the curious.

It is a town that lends itself to combustion; and most of the popular or unpopular leaders gave way to the temptation from the fifteenth to the eighteenth century. The rush of flame and fury up this groove of the mountains must indeed have been satisfactory; and one could see, when the superstructure had been thus removed, the ducats of the burghers gleaming among the blackened cellar-beams. Here and there a charred corpse lying, man or woman, it mattered little now; it is strange that this method of winding up accounts is still in vogue with nations.

The Austrians tramped down the high street in January 1849, glad to get out of the snows above and the harassings of the Körmöcz "rebels"; then the great war-drift floated away into the plain, and Selmeczbánya was saved this time from liquidation. On all this the tenth-century stronghold has looked down; but even its walls are hidden in the mountain-groove. The sun lights first upon the chapel of Calvary, when all the town is still and dark and grey; and, as it sets, the two white towers glow, first gold, then crimson, against the warm blue of the midland night.

We became familiar with Selmeczbánya. We rode down the rough ways of Lenge and Skleno—where are hotels and baths and waiters—and along under the cliffs of yellow and roseate lavas, which weather into tender purple as they rise in bluffs and spurs above the birch-woods. We collected enthusiastically at the superb cliff of natural glass, where old Beudant and many another worker have found their hearts' desire; and we asked one another if a geologist need go as far as the Yellowstone Park if he yearns for volcanic marvels. Below, as the Hlinik road emerges on the Garam, with its broad flat meadows and uncertain dusty banks, the rhyolitic lavas show fluidal and other structures in perfection. It was curious to think of these viscid masses flowing down into the hollows in recent geological times; but the river has got the better of them, and has carved its way across them unconcernedly, giving us the band of purple cliffs that flanks the green alluvium.

We entered Hlinik under the young moon, and received a wild ovation from the children, some fifty of whom pursued us down the road. This was too much for other forms of village life, and in a moment the street was a scene of wild confusion. These wide thoroughfares, like the Piazza della Signoria or old Cornhill, seem planned for popular agitation. A horse broke loose from a side alley; seven hairy pigs rushed tumultuously through a flock of geese; and black and brown cattle, otherwise most orderly, caracoled in all directions. It was a proud and stirring moment, and brought every one to his door. Waving a courteous adieu, we rode out with dignity, and again took to the dark highlands.

Thus we came to Vihnye, which we visited on a later occasion by daylight—a pretty bathing-resort at the foot of the forest-ridge; long may it be before these charming places are overgrown with guides and porters and streets of vast hotels! In all these narrow valleys the white cottages of the miners show at intervals among the pines; at night, when you are growing familiar with the starlight, and can just discern the tree-stems against the rocks, you will come upon a yellow lantern swinging before some little shrine; perhaps it is fastened to a tree, or is nailed high up against the scar; but through it the darkness, to many a traveller, becomes no longer fearful. And it is no easy matter to keep these lanterns lighted, nor is there a collection afterwards. Even where, by rates and taxes, we have given ourselves paved pathways and electric lights, we might hesitate to add on a penny in the pound for wayfarers whom we neither see nor know. Perhaps the air of cities deadens us; we have forgotten the starlight, and the night wind, and the pines.

Sometimes in the woodlands, as you rise slowly to the divide, and all sign of life seems left behind you, you may hear the sound of automatic ore-sifters away up some side-creek in the darkness—a strange, heavy, monotonous pounding, going on steadily as the unwatched water flows; until you can fancy the gnomes again at work among the caverns, with spade and pickaxe and undiminished laughter, pushing across the rubbish-heaps and falling over one another, in their haste to do a little work ere morning.

Another day, thanks to the generous kindness and good-fellowship of Dr. Cseh, the Government Geologist, we went into the huge silver-mine of the Schöpferstollen, where a locomotive and a train of wagons run in and out of the mountain-side. Guided by one of the managers, with two little Slovak lantern-boys before us, we walked among the sulphide-lodes for two and a half hours—a vast clean mine, with dry walls, and high roofs almost everywhere. The pretty group of offices at the entrance, in the style of

Grindelwald, would make the veriest outsider fall in love with mining.

As we emerged, we met the "shift" of workmen coming in, every one ready with the old salute "Glück auf!" a tradition from the Saxon miners. And then, looking down the

Market Place
Selmeczbánya
Hungary

hanging wall of the lode, we could see the outgoing shift climbing towards us in this slit-like excavation of the mountain, each man with his lamp slowly moving, like a vast company of glow-worms. From time to time the dull roar of blasting rose from the lower tunnels, and smoke choked our farther progress.

This, however, was down in the vale of

Hodrus. In Selmeczbánya itself we had our mineral museum and our town-excitements—the busy market, overflowing with huge green pumpkins, and laughing girls, and energetic old ladies, each intent on carrying the largest bundle in the world. The oxen of the district are superb white creatures, with horns three feet long, pulling from the neck like horses, and carrying their heads proudly and erect. Another zoological feature was a tame deer, which wandered casually in the corridors of *The Grapes*. This provincial old hotel let us very much alone; but one evening, as we returned by rail from Körmöczbánya, a man of solidity and solemnity appeared, seated in our dining-room, but eating nothing. When we had reached our coffee he rose and said he would like a word with us.

"I am," said he, "a commissary of police."

Contrary to the traditions of his office, he did not ask us to withdraw to his carriage and introduce us to his two gendarmes; but his manner was none the less worthy of *Monte Cristo*. Of course our passports, and a word about our good friend Dr. Cseh, maintained the tranquillity of nations; but the matter is worth mentioning, as Hungarians themselves believe that papers need not be carried in their country. The rule for all travellers, and especially for cyclists and pedestrians, is never to leave home without a passport, bearing at least one recent *visa*. The courtesy implied by its production is a far better way of maintaining the reputation of one's country than the traditional bluster of the

Ox-cart Skleno

" British subject " and a dozen of letters to *The Times*.

We were free from Selmeczbánya on a certain evening, and made a few miles westward out of a sense of duty, stopping at the simple inn of Hodrusbánya (Hodritsch). It is always hard work over that divide, and walking both up and down for the majority of cyclists. The inn, as is common in this simple country, has neither sign nor bush to advertise it, and is only to be known by an ox-wagon or two waiting patiently for the drivers. Our evening there was a gay one, with a great deal of talk from a lucidly-intoxicated mine-officer. Dashing young bravos, in slouch hats and black moustaches, came in and out, and secretly presented us with silver ore, with as much mystery as if the whole village would be proscribed on its becoming known. The mine-officer was very anxious, on a wet night and at 10 p.m., that we should come out and call upon his wife.

"She will be delighted," he said, somewhat thickly; "she speaks English, for she is a Frenchwoman."

I expressed my desire to see her more at her convenience; but why should she speak English?

"Ah," he said, "of course she does—French and English—it is all the same—of course it is."

This idea is common enough if one goes sufficiently far east to find it. As a matter of fact, we know deplorably little about the language of any one beyond the fifteenth meridian; why should they know more of us? Can all the kindly readers of these pages say what ordinary men speak in a land as near us as Moravia?

Our conversational miner raised another question of interest.

"English may be spoken in England," he admitted; "but in London, or Paris, you would naturally speak German. How would you understand one another otherwise?"

In Hungary, German has, within this century, replaced Latin as the language of intercourse among strangers; being entirely foreign to the people who speak it so politely, it seems to them a heaven-sent Volapuk. More than once we were attacked on this point—of course every one in London knew German; but English might be convenient in out-of-the-way country districts. Let us frankly admit the truth underlying this idea; for German, that mystery of magnificence and pathos, loved of *littérateurs* and set at nought by schoolboys, carries one at present over more ground in Europe than any other tongue.

Our friends in the little room at Hodrus introduced us to a small mild man from Philadelphia, who had resided in America for six weeks. We bowed, and he bowed; but he could speak nothing but Slovakish. Had the States rejected him; or had he wiped the dust of competition from his feet? He looked much more at home listening to his birth-companions across his beer, and smiling gently at the mention of the West, as if he kept all those secrets of Philadelphia to himself.

"England—America," repeated the lively mine-officer. We bowed across the table, regretting that we could not wave our respective banners.

Finally, just at 10 p.m., the night watchman came in for a preparatory draught. He is a functionary here, as in most combustible mountain-villages, and calls out good and charitable words in the gentle watches of the night. At Hodrus he was a singularly meek person, almost rivalling the Philadelphian; with his swinging lantern and his sixteenth-century halberd, he would have made a most admirable Verges.

Let us hope that his beer sustained him; for he girded his long coat at the waist, sighed deeply, and went out into as wet a night as any highland may desire.

AGAINST THE PLAINS

Time's glory is to calm contending kings,
To wake the morn, and sentinel the night,
To wrong the wronger till he render right.
       SHAKSPERE. *Lucrece.*

AFTER our visit to the Schöpferstollen, we went merely a few miles farther down the muddy valley, and crossed the Garam to Zsarnócza. One so seldom gets a written bill in Hungary, that I venture to record this of the spacious and well-served house in which we stayed.

	Fl. Kr.
Szoba (Room)	1 ·20
Gyertya (Candles)	·15
Vacsora (Supper)	·72
Kavé (Coffee)	·32
Bor viz (Wine water, *i.e.* mineral water) .	·12
Reggeli (Breakfast)	·92
	3·43

The total for one person is thus again well within three shillings.

The descent of the Garam had a spice of

novelty; but the roads were rutty and set with many stones. We were leaving the forest-ridges and approaching the vast alluvium of the plain. The term "Salisbury Plain" has long been known to cyclists as an excellent practical joke; similarly the Hungarian plain is by no means a level surface. The vast basin, some three hundred miles across, is full of the scourings of the mountains round it, and smaller streams cut deeply into the terraces of gravel and yellow earth which ancient rivers have brought down. The deposition, moreover, in so wide an area has naturally been unequal; and tumbled hillocks hundreds of feet in height have accumulated on the flanks of the Karpathians. Away near Budapest and Szegedin old floods may have levelled out the débris, giving one the strangely fascinating landscape that seems to stretch throughout all space. An evening on the citadel-platform at Buda, with the Danube emerging from the dark hills on the north, and winding away southward to Belgrade, everything, even the gilt and domed cathedral, now vague and soft in a brown haze—this will go far to make a man believe in plains. The coarse stream-heaps of the Garam and the Vág are very different, the mere fringes of the Magyar country, across which we climbed to-day, and from which we still looked down on the fenced cities of the plain.

At Garam-Szent-Benedek there is a noble two-spired church upon a platform, like so many in this country; and here we left the valley. The neat air of well-planed timber had departed as we descended from the highlands; the roofs

Garam-Szent-Benedek
Hungary

here were rudely thatched, lumpy and grown over like old gardens; and beside each house stood the long well-pole and weighted beam, characteristic of dry Eastern lands. The counterpoise of the beam is commonly a great stone tied on to it, and the bucket is carried by a pole suspended from the other end. At Szent-Benedek the post supporting the beam stands in the public footpath, and the pole hangs over into the private well in the stable-yard.

The road between the two rows of whitened one-storied houses is vaguely wide, as usual, and lambs and geese and children lose their way in it. The population gradually gathered to see us off, a wonderfully pretty piece of colour in the burning sunlight. Even a dainty crowd upon the stage seems lifeless after these Hungarian days.

A far better road, firm and hard, led us over the plateau to the west, up and down on a windswept open country, with the broken band of mountains above Nyitra as a background, and glimpses of blue hills beyond the Danube valley in the south. We were travelling, not "in the print of olden wars," but in that of very modern ones; for this country, less than fifty years ago, was literally ablaze with invasion and revolt. The air was black with smoke for weeks together, and the hot nights were lit up with long ripples of flame on the horizon, where, down at Komárom, farms, villages, boats, and bridges all flared together under the roll of Klapka's guns. For five months Komárom (Komorn) held out, a month after Görgei had handed over his 23,000 men to the Russians at Vilagós. Klapka's defence had roused echoes among all the enemies of Austria, just and unjust—and they were many; and the news of his enthusiastic reception in a theatre at Hamburg a fortnight later reads in strange contrast to the hanging and shooting of his fellow-generals which was going on briskly in Arad and in Pest. On Klapka in Hamburg and Görgei pensioned at Klagenfurt, survivors of this bitter whirlwind, the mind dwells thoughtfully to-day. The one man went on slaying, and is for ever the "hero of Komorn"; the other closed the struggle quietly, and is a name one does not care to breathe beyond Vienna. The facts of war are so intensely barbarous that a time may come when we shall cease to distinguish between soldiers; but at present, I fear even the coldest of us feels some thrill of battle as he rides through the cornland towards Nyitra.

"Nothing," wrote the *Times* correspondent in those fighting days, eminently correct and unemotional, "nothing can be more disgusting than the conceit of nationality"—a dictum not unheard of in our own time. But it is no surprise to find the same authority, a few weeks later, calling Bem "the indefatigable chief," and Görgei "that gallant officer." The quarrel had begun between Croats and Magyars; but now the infection spread, and democratic Hungary, attacked by empires, became the France of eastern Europe. Slovaks, Viennese, Italians forgave her; she was loved, and Russia feared her. What wonder, then, if some faint tremor became felt at last in the foundations of Pall Mall and Piccadilly?

And now, if trouble looms again—well, it will not be from the arrogance of Hapsburgism, which is washed and white as any lamb. Let us pull up for our mid-day bread in the little village of Csárad; we need not look farther than the sunshine of the present peace.

Csárad boasts of a fashion of its own, limited to girls of about twelve and under. The hair, soft and golden, is drawn close to the head as a sort of skull-cap, and is plaited in a tail behind; but a mysterious plait runs from this all round the brow—a neat edging, to undo which is an exercise in the fourth dimension. It has a quaint prim effect on these laughing children, as they cluster round us and feel the rubber of our tyres. They all carry light switches to drive geese with, until they are promoted to the coloured kerchief and the carrying of an infant brother.

When we swung down later into Aranyos Márot, we found almost a town, and were amazed at the military, and the square, and the hotel, and the public buildings; it was the sort of thing you expect to find in France, spotless in its stucco and distemper. The united commercial classes assembled in a little inn, and besought us not to go by Ghymes, but rather by a route ten miles to the south. The abomination of Ghymes appeared to be hills, which cyclists are supposed to hold in horror; and I am bound to say that the southern road was undulating enough before it ended. When we came to the last brow between Verebély and Nyitra (Neutra), we had one of the great scenes of the tour. There was a light air in the acacias that lined the roadway; the moon was golden above the wealth of cornfields, which spread in pale bronze across the hills; and below was a gleam of water, with the castellated pile and spires of Nyitra black against the last green twilight. And when we steered in among the female population and the garrison, and found the *Hôtel Szarvashoz (zum goldenen Hirschen)*, and sat at dinner in the garden, with lights on the table and the acacias over us—then all the air of the south was round us, and Krakow and the Tátra lay almost forgotten across the hills.

When we went up the fine limestone road next morning, we were on a route well followed by old travellers. Over it the observant Dr. Richard Bright was driven in his post-cart in 1815, amid the "submissive bows" of "wild and uncultivated" peasants. And over it M. Beudant walked some three years later, noting the sand-hills, and the pebbles, and all the

Dr. R. Bright in his Travelling-Carriage in 1815.
("*Travels in Lower Hungary,*" chap. iii.)

detritus of the mountains, like a good geologist, and manfully braving the great sun. He also came to the *Cerf d'or*, and was unceremoniously turned away into the street; pedestrians were far beneath the notice of an innkeeper in those days. Indeed, this energetic pioneer had to show his papers to a judge before he could get a room and a dinner in the town, whereon he remarks, with the fine humour of a Frenchman, "*Il en résulte que jamais une personne, capable de manger un poulet, ne s'avise d'aller à pied."*

Beudant went on by Ghymes, and so into the Garam valley, and up among the highland mines. His handsome quartos on the *Voyage en Hongrie* are pleasant reading nowadays, if only to note the changes of conditions. But his maxim for travellers holds good for all time; he could not understand how people complained about the peasantry—he always found them most obliging. "*La manière d'être reçu,*" quoth he very wisely, "*dépend beaucoup de la manière dont on se présente.*" At Ghymes he was received in the castle of the Count of Forgacs; and a damsel came forth and kissed his hand, to which he admits he was unaccustomed. Clearly Ghymes had better manners than lofty and episcopal Nyitra.

The new knights-errant of the wheel have, indeed, delightful kinship with their grandfathers, who told their travellers' tales in four volumes quarto and brown calf. The peasant is to cyclists a living personality; we may see how he adapts himself to his surroundings, how he varies from one valley to another, how the country lives in him and by his labour; we sit with him at the plain deal table of an inn, and lament not the swallow-tails and shirt-fronts of Lucerne.

Above Nyitra we saw men and women busy everywhere with the corn-stacks or the threshing, or cutting the grand green masses of the maize, and carrying it, like moving bowers, down the road. The farms, with their one-storied, red-roofed homesteads, are typical and enormous; the fields seem to go in waves across the horizon, and in one place they were being already ploughed by steam-machinery. This activity recalled the quays of Budapest, where agricultural machines, turned out in heaps from the barges of the Danube, form a sort of ornamental selvage to the town.

Then we came down to the Vág at Galgócz (Freistadtl), and found an odd little swimming-bath in the stream. Two bright boys also bathed with us, chiefly with a view to satisfying their curiosity about the machines. "Surely," said one of them, " you must eat a great deal on such a journey." "We do," we answered fervently.

Somewhere in the fen between this and the village of Lipótvár lies a fortress that was built as a bulwark against the Turks, but which was the first to make matters look serious in '49. To-day it is hidden among pleasant belts of trees. After a week's siege Leopoldstadtl became famous; and when the Austrian wounded began to come into Tyrnau from the frozen meadows of the Vág, people shook their heads and felt that Kossuth was in earnest. A month later the surrender was a blow to the imperialists. Here is an actual letter of the war-time:— "The garrison, after all their gasconading, behaved most pitifully, and their capitulation terribly disappointed our brave fellows, who had hoped that the fortress would be stormed, in which case their declared intention of 'not leaving man or mouse alive' would most certainly have been put into execution." It does no harm to reprint things of this kind; the style is common property among the black-coated gentlemen who take their fighting with their morning-coffee; and we had enough of it during the Indian "Mutiny," for one example, to know that it may be applauded by every Christian people.

Broad and sunlit, like the airy heart of France, the fields stretched away towards the towers of Tyrnau, or Nagy Szombat, as we call it in these times of compromise and peace. The resemblance to many a bright townlet *en province* must have struck M. Beudant also, when he admired the green shutters and the white-washed walls, and found the "*ensemble assez riant.*" Certainly we met with a hospitable reception. Officers, aged priests, shopkeepers, and waiters conspired to wish us the blessings of earth or heaven. I do not think we saw a wheeled vehicle in the streets, Nagy Szombat in this resembling our own cathedral towns; and this sobriety allows of freer conversation. We halted under the tall cathedral, with its two bulbous towers; a new kind of bulb grows here, by the bye, delicately flattened at the sides. Soon a citizen approached, willing to instruct us; we need not fear here the "guide" of western cities.

"Are you Christians?" he said—an enquiry not uncommon in the East; "or you are Germans, perhaps—probably Lutherans?"

Well, we were English, and we might be Lutherans.

"Ah," he said, to reassure us, "there are several Lutherans in this town." And then he took us into the cathedral, a plain white building of the fourteenth century, the chief quaintness of which lies truly in its modern towers.

When we sat later in a side street, under the awning of a café, and drank bumpers of green tea, we nearly filled the roadway with friendly citizens, and the police had to keep an eye on the popular demonstration from a distance.

That evening we felt some loss of spirit, for we faced the north again, and when should we return to Hungary? In the broad level light of sunset, a vast orange glow behind the forests of the Karpathians, and with the full moon behind us dimmed by the dust of the high road, we ran finally to Béláház. At Istvánlak, a village of mud houses neatly painted, we entered with the evening droves of pigs; and it was amusing to see how each pair chose out its proper house, grunting joyously at the door until it was opened. The geese, driven by demure little maidens with long sticks or well-directed whips, were enthusiastic at the arrival of the strangers. Flock mingled with flock, and flew geesefully down the road like a tornado. The pigs executed a *sauve qui peut* before them. The air was full of birds, and how they were sorted out again I know not.

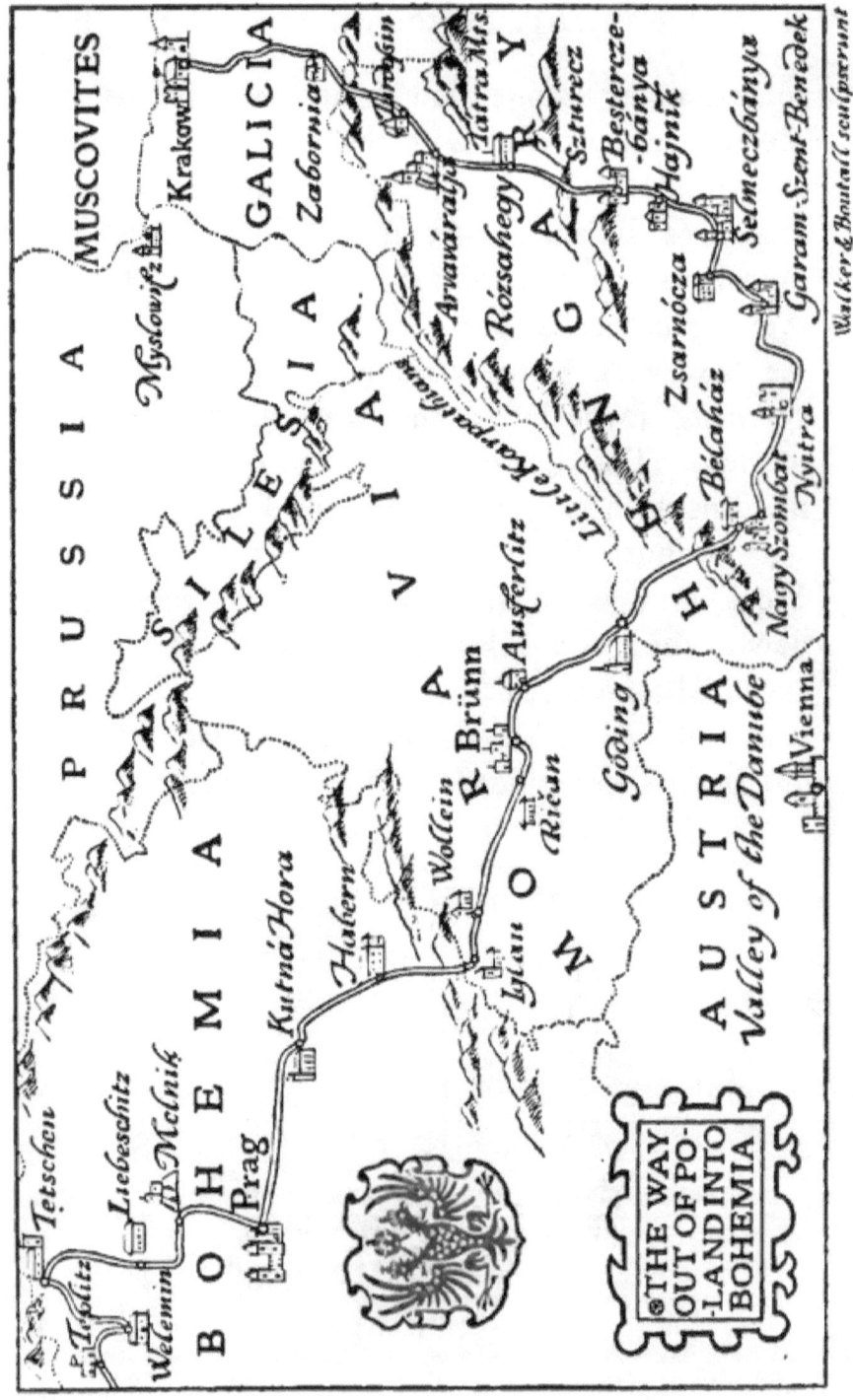

WE INVADE MORAVIA

>Stretched aloft and adown I see
>Two roads that part in waste country :
>The hills are a weary waste to wage ;
>But what of the valley-road's presage?
>That way must tend his pilgrimage.
>
>>ROSSETTI. *Rose Mary.*

N a bend of the road at Béláház we found our inn, more by the people going into it than by any sign. Though we are told that this is a "Slavisch" district, our young Jewish host and hostess are fluent in German; the beard of the man speaks his nationality, all the peasants being clean-shaven. Stolid old fellows they are, as they crowd into the house and take a drink on the way home. It is the custom for each man to write down his reckoning in a book kept by the landlord, the customer thus acknowledging his debt. Similarly I had to write out our own bill next morning, the figures being dictated by our host, so that it had all the solemnity of a contract. When you come to think of it, this is not a bad way of doing business; you can dispute the odd kreuzers as long as your

heart desires; your host feels bound to make explanations, why, for instance, your breakfast has cost 7d. instead of 6d.; and, when you have accepted the 7d., down it goes in your own handwriting, ready to rise up against you even in the day of judgment.

The burly peasants filed out slowly, several of them prudently inspecting their scores before leaving. The native hat is here reduced to the smallest possible dimensions, almost brimless, and interferes little with the massive roundness of the skull. There is something of an antique style about these stout straight-mouthed labourers. We were now back again in the solid old Slavonic ring.

Our suave young host asked for my passport, and locked it up for the night, professing that the police might want it. Politeness probably prevented him from suggesting that we might fly away without settling our account. He trusted the Observer, however, whom he probably regarded as a magnate. The Observer is a man of firmness—you can see it at a glance.

Then barefooted Katerina unwound the chain that went out through a hole in the wall of our sitting-room, and lowered the turnpike-pole across the road. The way to Moravia was thus secured. There was something quaint in this;

in much the same way the German knights once thought they could keep out Napoleon. Then, through the great room where the machines were stabled, and across the paved entry of the court, we went peacefully to our beds.

Next day being the Sabbath, our host apologised for putting only cold food before us; but he produced genuine *szalámi*—observe the spelling of the country—such as one gets in the mountain-huts of Tyrol. And then there were the unfailing cool green gherkins, which are taken out to the fields in glass jars full of vinegar, and which seem the staple commodity of many country markets. And of course there was the beautiful scarlet pepper—why have I not dilated on this before?—which we were to exchange this day for the coarse brown substitute of the west. When one has seen, day after day, the bright red *paprika* and the white salt side by side upon one's table, one feels an æsthetic want even in the most polite society. I would go back to the plain boards of these Hungarian inns at any moment with delight; and the room would be cool as we sit at our simple breakfast; but outside the great sun is waiting for us above the gleaming highway, and we would face him morning after morning, steering for the Roman east.

It was clear and hot already when Katerina swung open the great carriage-doors, and let us out abruptly into the customary flocks of geese, which were this time outward bound. At Nadas, a very well kept village, its houses gay with white, blue, and yellow ornamental bands, we were already high on the Little Karpathian slope. The push beyond proved exceeding rough and steep, and so was all the forest ridge. We enjoyed one great view—our last—of the Danube valley, and then plunged down, over titanic road-metal, towards the Moravian border. Here again we were crossing the axis of central Europe; but the granite core is still covered up by massive Miocene conglomerates. It is wonderful what an amount of rock has to be cut away before you can make a decently artistic mountain.

As we looked behind us, after coming down a track that was more like a stream-bed than a road, the grand tower of Schartenstein dominated the forest-slopes, one of the last Hungarian outposts. We were now in a busy cornland, with bright market-towns; and the women, in red and orange bodices and gay kerchiefs, with high boots and short blue skirts, formed brilliant patches of colour in the streets. The men who came and went under the arches of the stableyards were embroidered all over, up and down, as if to keep the girls in countenance.

The road from Szenicz is quaintly carved by wagons out of the soft alluvial dust, just as the deep yellow lanes in Surrey have been cut by Roman traffic rather than by English engineers. A great castle appeared to northward, stranded in the cornfields; then we made our last descent, and struck the Morava at Holic.

The Morava sounds so much prettier than the March; but we cannot undertake to use Slavonic names all across Moravia and Bohemia. Some districts are so German that to revert to the Tchech forms would seem pure pedantry; others are so Tchech that to employ German would be an insult. I think we will be German in Moravia—for the most part.

Crowds of women and girls were coming into Holic along the grand avenue of poplars; there must have been a market at Göding across the frontier. The way for two miles was simply bright with them, all in their best and prettiest array. We saw later, however, what a hard time they must have of it to compete with the toilets of Moravia.

The Morava is a feeble and adulterated stream; but the Observer, as is his wont, enthusiastically bathed in it; and I followed also, glad to escape from the mosquitoes. A friendly young man guided us to the bathing-place, and conversed with us from the bank. After dinner at the *Hôtel Kopper*, he brought round some eight members of the local cycling club to express the cordiality of Göding; and we discussed the sport, and the trade of Great Britain, and the sugar-factories of Göding, as we promenaded up and down the pavements, with a golden moon smiling on us along the deserted street.

Two of these Moravian brothers looked in again at the start next morning. I said we wished to go by Austerlitz.

"Oh no," said one, "the main road to Brünn is far better; besides, what is there to see at Austerlitz?"

"Well, it is interesting, is it not?"

"No, no, quite a little place, I assure you."

"But it is spoken of in history?" I urged.

"*So?*" replied the youth of Göding, with affected incredulity.

Then I recollected that the Austrians may not be quite so interested in Austerlitz. Even this Grand Duchy of Moravia, with its Tchech language and affinities, is not quite lost to a sense of federal decency. My morbid curiosity stood rebuked.

None the less, of course, we went by Austerlitz. Slavkov is said to be the native name, and may prove convenient as a euphemism; I reserve it for Grand Dukes, diplomats, and imperialists.

It was a Sunday. The road from Göding went at first very vilely through a wood, and then blossomed out into a genuine *Kaiserstrasse*, grey and solid and imperial, a road for cannon. Two quaint little coal-mines appeared on the crest of a hill, a heap of coal and a wooden hut representing the whole industry, in the midst of an innocent ploughed field.

Public notices are posted up in Tchech—this strikes me as a neater word than "Czech," and is truer to the sound; or you may write it "Chekh," as M. Leger and Mrs. Hill do in that admirable but oddly-named book, *A History of Austro-Hungary*. And to-day the Tchech costumes were more elaborate than anything we had seen in Hungary or Poland. The young men of Tscheitsch might have walked off the boards of a very pretty comic opera, with their white shirts, a brilliant little vest, embroidered in scarlet and gold, reaching just below the chest, and a dark sleeveless jacket over it, with gleaming rows of buttons. The hat is also dark, low-crowned, and almost brimless, with a gay wreath of solidly-worked flowers round it, and a couple of long white cock's feathers rising, high and graceful, at the side.

At Nasedlowitz we met the peasants coming from a church amid the woods; and here the young men's hats were covered with metallic-looking beads, while the elders had high-crowned puritanic ones of plain black straw. But the women excelled in splendour, with short expanded skirts of vivid pink, or rich green, or white, or lustrous black, on which reposed daintily-coloured aprons. Some strode along in the great Hungarian boots; and many wore silver corselets about their strong full figures, gleaming like unproved armour. These metal plates were bound about with scarlet, and the neck above was hidden in a true Elizabethan ruff. The head-kerchiefs were mostly dark, with coloured spots and borders; but favour was also given to a splendid orange. Truly, untrodden Moravia has retained its simplicity of life.

To see the throng passing among the trees, or across the background of dull brown fields, from which the corn had been cut already, or against the long green strips of maize, had the effect of a procession of iridescent gems. It was startlingly beautiful, and it was all true; Marie had dressed for Moric here, and not for any crowd of summer visitors.

Under copper-coloured clouds, with one great thunderous burst of rain, we came over the last brow and saw below us Austerlitz—a row of poplars on the high road, the white village gleaming from between them, and beyond it the bank of the Littava, cultivated in long brown fields. A little chapel caught the sunlight on the crest; and then there were folds of blue hills and woodlands in the north. Some ninety years ago, when the snow was on these summits, and the meadow-land was frozen over, 150,000 men, French and Austrian and Russian, had looked upon this landscape, and had then, at the bidding of a few fur-clad and be-ribboned individuals, proceeded to tear each other piecemeal. Such affairs will seem ridiculous as time goes on, when we can forget the bitter blindness, the wild mad tragedy of it all.

It was somewhere hereabouts, after the defeat, that young Rostof met his sovereign, and was afraid to speak to him, "just as a young man in love trembles, not daring to say what he has been dreaming about night after night." Away on the left Prince Andrei lay, and saw for the first time the infinite greatness of the sky, "immeasurably lofty, and with light grey clouds slowly wandering over it." We may look in our Alison for the official records, and yet come back to the histology of affairs in Tolstoi's *War and Peace*. Nowadays, as we run down on Austerlitz, we cannot help thinking of Prince Andrei, and how, in his supreme moment, Napoleon appeared to him so very insignificant after all. There is, indeed, little trace of the Emperor, for good or ill, to-day between the Vistula and the Rhine.

The field of battle lay below us as we passed the white mediæval gateway, climbed the bank of the Littava, and struck the vastly undulating road along the crest. Here some friendly cyclists spied us, and waited to escort us into Brünn. In the evening, from our palatial quarters in the *Grand Hôtel*, we met the Club by invitation in a garden-restaurant, and took tea and lemons from 9.30 to 11. This Club admitted Jews, a fact that caused another one to flourish which excluded them. Our friends were bright gentlemanly brothers of the wheel, and had recently entertained a few members of the famous *Hunnia* Club of Budapest. When they found that I had sat in Pest at the weekly supper of the *Hunnia*, in their modest retreat in Great-Nut-Tree Street, our bonds of sympathy became close indeed. Sport is a great humaniser, when lower animals are not dragged into it; and to-day the name of "Beeston-Humber" is an introduction to the capitals of Europe.

Brünn, or Brno, if you prefer it, is situated on the Schwarzawa, and contains some 90,000 inhabitants. Also many chimneys, and huge factories, and a towerless cathedral, and several strangely spine-like spires. But the smoke of enterprise cannot dull the great golden cornfields, wave on wave around the town; or the long yellow castle on the "*infausta rocca di Spielberg,*" where Pellico lay chained eight years. Brünn now speaks of Pellico freely, and the social revolution has marched in our day in its streets. A city so familiar with the conquerors of the Austrians has become somewhat largely tolerant; and its reception of the Prussians in 1866 was at any rate not on the Moscow model. The more one wanders through what is called, with pleasant irony, the Austrian Empire, the more one realises that the fabric, like the mercury in a barometer, is maintained by pressure from without.

We had two more nights in Moravia—one at Ričan (pronounced Ritchan), a straggling village, where our host was dark and dignified as a count in exile; and we felt awkward at seeing him removing plates or carrying water to our rooms. But we were nearing Bohemia, and this quality of refinement arose, in all probability, from his being the local butcher. Things in

Bohemia have a touch of Araby, and not of any rational modern land.

Thenceforward we had a trim prosperous country of villages emulating small towns, with public schools and official residences, neatly painted, and gleaming in a cloudless air; and fir-woods on the intervening ridges, with a strip of grass or oat-field between the dark tree-stems and the road. And the road itself was lined with mountain-ashes, now in full glory of scarlet berries and delicate grey-green leaves. Every stream-cut showed the old floor of gneiss and granite, the floor of Europe, with a dry peat soil above it, soft and springy to the wheel.

Amusing guesses were made at our nationality in a country where so few Englishmen are seen. In Hungary, having come from Krakow, we were commonly regarded as Poles; on second thoughts it was suggested that we were Frenchmen. The Observer was one day taken for a Bohemian, whereon he at once went and had his hair cut. Hence in the Tchech district we were not concealed, even by protective mimicry; and the two English cyclists were as great a wonder as Patagonians.

There is one solid advantage, however, in these romantic countries—no one ever comments on your costume. It is presumed to be that of your own district, somewhere over the watershed yonder, just as your language is a German or Slavonic pâtois. The little boys at Milan or Verona, brought up to worship the frock-coat of Cavour, are by no means so tolerant of British tweeds and knickerbockers.

Our last Moravian evening was at Wollein, where we halted in the rain; and here our entertainer was a Viennese. But where could one wish for a brighter or a better hostess than the *wohlgeborene Frau Rosa Klauda*, as she was styled in a testimonial on the wall? Round and smiling and attractive, she ran in from the kitchen to the fine bright bar-room at every creak of the entrance-door, and kept her two barefooted native damsels on the alert. She had caused ivy to grow in pots on the window sills, and had trained it in live festoons around the pictures and along the walls; her rooms, with their light-coloured furniture, reminded one of a first-class coffee-house in England; and she explained all this neatness and briskness by the fact that she had once come with her husband on business to Wollein, and had found no decent place to stay in. They resolved that the scandal should at once be rectified.

"I am not really an innkeeper's wife," she

would say; "I was born in Vienna—it was quite different there, you understand."

But no innkeeper, we thought, had ever better fortune. The grave proprietor went about leisurely, and at times cut wood in the back-yard; he had other business in hand. But it was clearly Frau Rosa who kept the Klauda Gasthaus.

"You will not forget us?" she said, as she saw us off next morning; "you will put Wollein in your book?" For she had seen us writing up our diaries.

And we made a sketch of the house, spacious and elegantly gabled, with ZÁJEZDNÝ HOSTINEC, "Accommodation for man and beast,"[1] written boldly down one side.

[1] Literally, "Traveller's Inn," the words implying travel with a horse or carriage.

The Klauda Gasthaus Wollein

UNTAMED BOHEMIA

> The Emperor shall not live but by my leave,
> Nor any potentate of Germany.
>
> MARLOWE. *Faustus.*

AND now for pure Bohemia, which we thought to take as an interlude in passing, but which quickly entangled us in its wiles. I am sure to make mistakes of fact or policy in dealing with Bohemian names, and shall be sternly German in the tourist-districts of the north. But the Tchech language is so charming when one has heard it, and the accents are so elegant on paper, that one cannot forego the chance of doing justice to one's friends ; and the whole of Bohemia seems friendly.

We did not come in for such a sheep-shearing as made the fortune of Autolycus ; perchance we were later in the season. But we certainly were destined to behold "bright Phoebus in his strength," and Bohemia only smiled the fairer. At the present time, as was spoken of her foster-child,

> Nothing she does or seems
> But smacks of something greater than herself;

a greater self that is yet to come, in the days of democracies and federations. Bohemia is just now in the unfortunate stage when crime shelters itself behind a national policy. It is not always remarked, as Dr. Johnson would say, that criminals, when they attack classes rather than individuals, show praiseworthy qualities of organisation, and should receive at least some of the credit given to Cromwell, or Frederick, or Napoleon, in the corresponding stages of their careers. The successful general, moreover, is supported by Government funds and a vast majority of public favour; your struggling revolutionary has not even the aid of a policeman. At any rate, it is high time to set crime upon a uniform basis of condemnation, and not to sing a *Te Deum* for an imperial hecatomb, and then put a rope round the neck of a political assassin.

The Tchech lands were thus in troublous days when we came into them, and they have been enjoying that sort of thing for at least six hundred years. A man shot by a fanatic for speaking German in the streets of Prag; great "national" riots at Iglau; cyclists overturned, also for being Germans, on the high road running into Brünn; and another enemy of the people attacked by furnace-hands, and incontinently beaten with hot irons. These are the penalties one pays for agitation, whether in favour of a popular preacher, a royal adventurer, or a national idea. The newspapers reported these events according to their predilections and their lights; but the native press was a sealed book to us, and we read only the German side. We were destined to see for ourselves in a day or two how high feeling actually ran.

We came over the hills to Iglau, Jihlava of the Tchechs, and gazed into unknown Bohemia. We fortified ourselves with dictionaries and phrase-books, so as to gather a few Slavonic crumbs; and a kindly schoolmaster assured us afterwards that the grammar of the language could be mastered in about fifty years. That was his experience from the peasants round him, who doubtless regarded him as exacting. Another philological lesson from an innkeeper showed us that the correct pronunciation of one letter, at least, out of the thirty-four, is still as debatable as the use of " h " in England.

A sentence or two from Terebelsky's *Lehrbuch*, suitable for cyclists, will not seem inappropriate. Like Japanese, there is a pictorial air about Bohemian, owing to the scattering of the accents. Thus :—

Je dobrá cesta? Is the road good?
Která je nejlepší hospoda? Which is the best inn?
Jsem celý promoklý. I am wet through entirely.
Přáli bychom si pokoj s dvéma postelema. We want a double-bedded room.

I spare the reader the usual anachronisms about pistols and post-horses, and the anecdotes of the Emperor Joseph II., in which all reputable phrase-books still abound. The above will be found sufficiently refreshing. The percentage of vowels in the quotations is almost the same in English as in Bohemian ; but their arrangement gives an elegance to the latter.

For those who are passing through a country, and who yet want some faint knowledge of common words, of the directions on signposts or the inscriptions of shop-windows, the most practical little books are a series published by E. Bock, Leipziger Strasse 37, Berlin. These are the "*Neue Sprachenführer*," in which various combinations of languages can be selected, the pages of each book exactly corresponding ; so that one can turn up the same sentence in German, Russian, Bohemian, Servian, or Hungarian, at a moment's notice. The price of 1m. 50pf. per volume commends them to the impecunious cyclist.

Thus we climbed the river-bank into

Bohemia, and found in our first town, Německý Brod (Deutsch Brod, the German Ford) a picturesque old centre of typically Bohemian taste. The native architects have traditions of their own—memories, perhaps, of the pre-Roman camps and the old beech-forest, which make them resent rule and uniformity. The centre-piece of the market-square of Německý Brod is a bold spouting fountain of allegorical design; in the corner is the church, with a tower of the grossest irregularity, even the clock being at one angle of it, and a gallery running round the top under an almost Norwegian wooden roof. Farther back, a Polish dome and bulb rise from the centre of the nave. All round, the fronts of the houses are like the wildest fantasy of a scene-painter. Classical forms are converted to Bohemian usage, and the sky-line of pediments is as broken as a wild sea-wave. Gables are in vogue, but they are treated in a humorously Palladian vein. A two-storied shop will thus have a façade like an Italian church, and dormers are run up, not with trim flanks and daintily projecting eaves, but with huge expanded wings of stucco. One becomes able in time, however, to distinguish a cottage from a cathedral. The market-place seems to beam with a quaint hilarity upon the traveller; one recognises a cheery fulsomeness—Bohemia is *assez riant.*

We sped out over the magnificent *Kaiserstrasse,* across the undulating gneissic plateau, and pulled up in a land of little pools and scattered tree-clumps at the *Sonne* Inn of Habern.

It was our first Bohemian night, and here we seemed to find the good old shepherd, with his
Pray you, bid
These unknown friends to us welcome.

The attentions of the house in this country are usually paid by the proprietor himself or by his son, who acts as head-waiter. There is no solemnity of service, but the host himself fills the glasses, or sends his son to the cellar for the clear brown *Pilsener*—or for the simple *Siphon* of the cyclist. The "head-waiter" strolls about in a short lounge-coat, perhaps with a cigarette between his lips; he sits down and chats with the visitors, or joins them at a game of billiards, every now and then performing some little service, as a man might in his family mansion. One would think it a matter of distinction to become an innkeeper in Bohemia.

The *Gasthaus zur Sonne* had a mediæval interior, such as lingers also in Tyrol and

Karinthia. The public rooms were narrow and stone-vaulted, and had the aspect of a resuscitated dungeon. Mr. R. L. Stevenson has raised the designs of the toy-theatre, the imagery of Skelt, to a fine art; but I am prepared to uphold those admirable drawings as examples of a rigid realism. They show far less of fantasy than of observation; and you need not go beyond Bohemia to pack a sketch-book full of Skeltery. The environment of *The Miller and his Men* expands before our eyes; the very trees are there, conveniently leafy at the wings; the crags are crowned with castles, long and red-roofed, the like of which never grew in sober England; and the village inns are fit at one moment for a carouse of harmony, at another for treasons, stratagems, and spoils. It was all again so delightfully true; Bohemia was Bohemian after all.

The village-schoolmaster has a social function in Bohemia. Round and cheery and comfortable withal, he receives strangers at the inn, and unburdens himself of courteous information. At Habern he did the honours of the country, and was proud to be asked about the hundred children in his care. While we dined and talked there, four musicians played and sang in the antechamber, and for the joy of it one might have been in Italy. No wonder that the nation clings to a language such as that.

Upon this scene of human kindness one expects to see Schabatzky, or Von Lindenbaum, or Golotsch, suddenly enter, "2nd dress." He carries two pistols, to render him less conspicuous, and here flings his cloak aside, revealing a cuirass studded with brass rivets and a belt of superhuman magnitude. The music ceases; the clouds of tobacco-smoke drift into the hollows of the roof.

"Ha, ha!" says Golotsch, or the other bravo; "carousing still, ye minions? Seraphina has escaped us (*the orchestra strikes a chord*). Hark there! the foe is at the gates!"

(*In the distance are heard the trumpets of the Swedes. Red fire to burn. The curtain falls.*)

Too often this highway has known the tramp of pikemen or the blustering throng of cavalry, stern-faced men of Prag, hunting down Catholics in the name of the Lord; or disciplined forces from Vienna, hanging on the outskirts of Bohemia, which flung them off hotly, or shut them up in Plzen or Jihlava; and the Hungarians, pious Romans for the nonce, coming over by our cycle-route from the dark Karpathians, sweeping up to Prag with banners flying, and then hurrying out again before the ungovernable Tchechs. In 1422 the blind patriot Žižka, whose name now stands for all that is national in Bohemia, had cleared the Emperor Sigismund out of Kutná Hora, tumbled his forces down into the Časlav road, pursued them away across the snow and the frozen ponds of Habern, and caught them up at Německý Brod, where the betrayal of the prophet Hus was in truth very bitterly avenged. Five years later, in defence of pure religion and undefiled, we find Prokop, the renegade priest, following up the invaders, and carrying the Hussite vanguard to the Danube. Forty years pass away, and the nation is still aflame with Christian zeal and charity; Mathias Corvinus, whom Vambéry has styled "the wealthiest and most luxurious ruler in all Europe," son of John Hunyadi, terror of the Turks, was trying his hand also in Bohemia. Like the faithless Sigismund, he was shattered on this granite upland, and worked off his troubles, with the Papal blessing, on more tractable victims in Moravia.

If we want, up and down the world, inspiration for a national outburst, surely we may find it between the German Ford and Prag; but there let us close the book, if we have any regard for Churches on one side or the other.

> That is thy Father's Altar, and thereon
> Blood-offering, brighter than the life of lambs,
> Is offered by His Priests.

The north wind is blowing keenly between the poplars, and the morning sky is cloudless; let us go down and take our bathe in the mere of Habern, and then away for Časlav.

The Rathhaus Goltsch-Jenikau

Cyclists on tour are still rare at Golčův Jenikov (Goltsch Jenikau), where we soon gathered a crowd around the fountain. I had to sit upon the machine to get any view of the quaint gabled houses, carried on elliptical arches, and the magnificently eccentric town hall, with a tower like a sprouting hyacinth. Ten miles away we could see the tall church-towers of Časlav, pale against the blue woods and long brown sunlit fields.

We had been advised to turn aside and visit Kutná Hora (Kuttenberg), an old silver-mining town on the slopes above the *Kaiserstrasse;* and into its narrow paved streets, higher and higher, we pushed between old carved stone houses, until we reached the level of the long palace, and halted at a patriarchal inn. We lunched in a great vaulted chamber, in the company of poetic and long-haired Bohemians of romance. The "waiter" was here a benign old gentleman in a smoking-cap, who was called away from the billiard-table on all sides, responding with equanimity to the commandant in full uniform, the embryo poet, and the cyclist.

We had come to see St. Barbara's, a grand unfinished enterprise of the fourteenth century, its tall interior once covered with frescoes, which a certain professor is now restoring. In the lower panels we have local industries, such as mining and assaying, with more spiritual scenes above them. These painted surfaces rise to some 80 or 100 feet in the side-chapels of the choir, and illuminated coats of arms appear even on the bosses of the ceiling. The customary whitewash covered this magnificence for many years.

This grand attempt in Gothic, reminding one of Beauvais, a choir and the east half of a nave, stands royally on the steep bank of the river; across the ravine one can see pale current-bedded sandstones, hung with bushes, supporting the old terraced town.

Another noble feature of Kutná Hora is a

church with a campanile, a real slender tower dominating a picturesque group of roofs and turrets, a welcome change from the bulbous enormities of the east. Many of the streets are narrow even for pedestrians, and end in steps and private passages. Let no one cycling on this historic highway pass by the branch to Kutná Hora.

We came out by Sedlec Abbey, now chiefly used as a tobacco-factory. The Observer's tyre loosened itself at Malin, just where we struck the *Kaiserstrasse*, and this diversion occupied him a gentle hour. He was touring with a new machine, which had all the merits of an Austrian plan of battle—absolute perfection if you got the enemy to agree to it. It must be admitted that the loose stones of Hungary and North Bohemia were enemies that stood on the offensive; and the Observer would attend to the wants of his "fifty-inch" from one to two hours daily, until we ceased to grumble at it, and found in it the tender interest of an ambulance. The Observer certainly does not stick at trifles; he would have stayed under that wall at Malin till the moon rose, rather than be beaten by a ring of *Gummi*, as the Germans quaintly call it.

We got under weigh again, and the road suddenly grew worse, as is customary in a prosperous industrial district. Let him refrain from cavilling who has laboured through South London or the Potteries. We struggled on, and struck the Elbe at Kolin, a town with a few fine Gothic houses and many fuming chimneys; and then we shot out in the cool twilight into another stretch of this undulating cultivated plateau. Those who can read it may find much about this spot in Carlyle; but *Frederick the Great* in ten volumes is more serious to some of us than Johnson's *Dictionary*, and the latter work is at any rate written in English. The details of the battle are all there, however, in book xviii. chapter iv., for those who take interest in "mortal engines." Plaňany and the other villages have picked themselves together since Carlyle inspected them; or did their squalor exist mainly in the eye of a man who abhorred "the nationalities," themselves "abhorrent of German speech"? On our right, as we rode westward, we had the old Prussian lines; on our left, the scene of the opening clash of cavalry, and Daun's position, which he held so unexpectedly that summer afternoon, the end of the matter being that he cannonaded the Prussians, not only out of the Kolin highway, but back across the Saxon frontier.

We could not stop with Daun among his batteries and sing praises for the slaughter; we pressed forward into Plaňany, which is now a large village, with a railway station and an air of business; and there we pulled up before the best hotel.

We found our way into the *salon*, which was full of the local men of leading and their wives and daughters—good-looking Bohemians enough; and the host, Teutonic of aspect, with his pipe and spectacles, chatted to them across the tobacco-smoke, and greeted the ladies with respectful gravity. A fine light-haired young man, presumably the son of the house, and about the handsomest fellow in the room, strolled around, playing the part of tapster, as Prince Henry may have done in the tavern of East Cheap. We asked the host modestly for rooms.

He shook his head, and contented himself with monosyllables of German. The guests looked round at us curiously, and we came to the conclusion that we were not understood. The house was so extensive that it seemed impossible it could be full. At last the Observer, always practical, plucked forth a Bohemian phrase-book.

His eloquence had no more effect. We were simply refused, and that was all.

We went across the way to a humbler inn, where they spoke German, but where they still declined to have anything to do with us.

"You will have to go a stage farther," said one man, somewhat brutally.

"To Böhmisch Brod?" I said. It was already growing dark, and the road was barely rideable.

We were puzzled; this was so utterly contrary to our general reception by the Tchechs. We went down the village and tried the smallest inn.

No; they could not give us even a single bed.

Then we felt that there was something underlying this, and we thought of applying at the police-station. Fortunately we dropped into the shop of an old general merchant, to whom we explained ourselves as English strangers; could he help us? He took a fatherly interest in us, and sent his boy to point out a hotel where he felt sure we should be received. As we expected, this was our old acquaintance, the *Hostinec na Rychtě*.

Prince Henry came to the door of it.

"We can find no room anywhere," we said; "cannot you manage something?" He looked at us, but did not answer.

"See what you can do," we urged; "we are English."

He replied by withdrawing into the *salon*, and we looked again towards the police-station.

Then the sedate host came out, and cautiously entered into a parley. After offering us one bed, he added, "But you are English?"

"We are," we said; "we are travelling from Krakow to Coblenz."

"So? We had taken you for Germans."

We laughed. "You ought to have let us speak a little longer; you would soon have found us out."

By this time the Prince and a number of the guests had come to the door to have a look at us.

"They are English," said the host, as if apologising for being caught in conversation.

"But can we have a bed?" we said; "one will be sufficient."

"Oh, come in," answered the host, "you shall have two beds; you shall have anything you like—the best room in the house. We had taken you for Germans. *Natürlich*, we do not speak German to Germans."

We were twenty-eight miles from Prag, and Bohemia has had seven hundred years of German rule. *Austria Felix* has not always imparted her felicity.

The guests expanded to us all at once; they insisted on dragging in the machines with their own hands, with more fervour than mechanical dexterity, and in stabling them in the great vaulted bedroom on the entrance-floor. I believe it was also a guest who brought us water and a towel. They crowded about us, all talking German fluently.

"Ah," they said, "of course we understand German; but we do not speak it to Germans."

This hospitable excitement gradually settled down again. Presently we were seated in the billiard-room and *salon*, the guests of young Bohemia; lemonade-bottles were discharged, and huge *Wiener Schnitzel* lay hot before us on the board.

At 11 p.m. we rose and bowed ourselves out, leaving our friends Bohemianly singing and keeping up the courage of the nation.

THE VOLCANIC ZONE

And we came to the Isle of Fire: we were lured by the light from afar,
For the peak sent up one league of fire to the Northern Star.
TENNYSON.   *The Voyage of Maeldune.*

IN the morning at Plaňany we were attended by the womenfolk only, and a visitor acted as our interpreter. We came easily to Český Brod (Böhmisch Brod), where the Utraquists and Taborites, the two divisions of the Hussites, not content with unhorsing the imperial cavalry and threshing out the foot with flails, quarrelled over the terms of peace, and so fell on one another. This was enough to weary Europe. Prokop and sixteen thousand Taborites were sacrificed by their fellow-reformers on a question of ecclesiastical compromise. But Europe refused to be wearied; she still had Magdeburg in store.

We left the granite upland, and came into the famous Silurian basin of Bohemia, across red grits and sandstones and steeply tilted shales.

At length, beyond the hot haze of the cornfields, we saw the towers of Prag—a grand Gothic group in the valley of the Moldau; and we hailed them gladly, as many invaders have done upon the Časlav road. But Prag can never recover her impressiveness until she extinguishes the factory-chimneys and compensates the porcelain-works, removing them to an airy distance. At present it is excellent to have a giant's strength, a national enthusiasm, to name a vast suburb Žižkov, and to crowd it with the ardent artisan; but to use it as a giant is another thing, and Prag as a place of beauty or of pleasure is impossible. Nothing saves you from the solid carbon particles; an open window is a doubtful luxury; and the superb mass of palace and cathedral across the river becomes majestic only in the evening, when the sun makes even the smoke-drift beautiful. Then the steep bank and the towers merge into one rich tint of brown; the sky grows lurid over them; you can scarcely see the water, gliding silently from bridge to bridge; and the Hradschin seems like an enchanted city, floating in an unholy glamour betwixt our earth and heaven. As you turn away from it and look up westward, you may catch some glimpse of the clear night air and of the stars.

If Prag, as we may hope in reason, is to

become the Bohemian Budapest, a good deal of her antiquity must suffer. Modern capitals require light and life, boulevards and spacious gardens. The new Museum is a fine beginning, and much old Gothic will finally go down before it, regretted more by those who visit the town than by those who have to live in it. So long as the towers are spared, with their high-pitched roofs and airy pinnacles, Prag will have a character of her own; and if the gloomy streets, that have seen so much turbulence and slaughter, float away into the past like old Paris, Rouen, or Cologne —— well, we may heave the poetic sigh and congratulate the sanitary engineer. Cities have to be cities, after all, and not museums; and if you want to see the triumph of a municipal council, to whom the clean sweep of revolution has given a free hand, you have only to go to the capital of the East, the new Byzantium on the Danube.

We visited the sights of Prag; but the towers of the Karlsbrücke seem the best embodiment of the city. When tired of observing this or that window, out of which the town-councillors were periodically cast, or of endeavouring to make up our minds about the Hussites, who flared through the annals for two centuries, we can come back to the west end of the bridge, and step right away from the nineteenth century to the days of Hus himself. Every form of sudden death, from stones to the crack of Prussian musketry, has crowded this narrow way with ghosts unknown to history; they swarm up from the river, in the shadow of these massive piers, silent, restless, unrequited; the evening deepens, till a last sun-burst touches on the topmost towers; and then we may see

> The cloud-rack parted, the cold north on fire,
> And all the gods, their cruel cheeks aflame,
> Thronging against the blacken'd bars of Heaven.

Those who go crusading with a cheerful countenance must find some answer to the visions of the bridge of Prag.

The famous Jewish cemetery, hidden away among the houses, takes one even out of mediævalism; the tombstones are crowded against one another, above graves in which the just lie four deep, elders of the seventh century serving as props for those of the seventeenth. Here one may still see a row of little pebbles laid respectfully on the tomb of a professor, a contemporary of Tycho Brahe; Prag itself is young in presence of such traditions and such a race.

In the Cathedral we beheld the vast shrine of St. John of Nepomuk, who figures as the

Becket of Bohemia—a monument of burnished silver, wild with angelic beings and eccentricities of a florid age. A silver life-size angel—if angels are the size of mortals—appears to float in air against a column of the gloomy aisle.

The chapel of good King Wenceslaus, who founded the Cathedral, was not built until the fourteenth century, some four hundred years after his murder; but it has all the grand air of ancient days. Above, one may see the faded frescoes that once covered all the upper panels, as far as the groining of the roof. But in the lower half the walls are inlaid with polished stones, of irregular outlines, set in coarse plaster—slabs from two to eight inches across, amethyst, red jasper, and clear green prase, nobly barbarian, imperishable as the works of saints.

In the quiet academic courts of the old Museum, Prof. Anton Frič, the friend of all geologists, planned a tour for us through the volcanoes of the north, and sent us out for another week of bright Bohemian days. Before we start on a new stage, let us note that Hungary, Moravia, and east Bohemia have all dealt kindly with us; it is twenty days since we left Krakow, and the total expenditure for one of us amounts to just £7.

So, on a burning afternoon—the sun had now started the campaign in earnest—we pushed out of Prag under the eye of the police, and mounted where permitted in the suburb. We climbed the bank, and that evening, after ferrying the Elbe, arrived in Melnik, where the church and castle stand on a bold bank of vines, descending to the united Elbe and Moldau. The inn of the young Čižek couple was of the usual clean and homely type, where the townsfolk, men and women, gather nightly to discuss society and beer. It had the airy character, with great basins and great bedrooms, to which the Tchech countries had accustomed us. Of course, for travellers' purposes, a village in Bohemia corresponds to a small town in Hungary, where the accommodation is much more limited. Moreover, one can conceive tragedies among those tall, grim, clean-shaven Slovak peasants; but in cheery Bohemia they lie far below the surface. The inn of Melnik was made as the centre of most honest comedy.

The schoolmaster was again to the fore, in his faultless suit of black; but even this can be worn with gaiety.

"The gentlemen speak *Platt-Deutsch?*" he said politely, noticing our accent.

"No, *Englisch-Deutsch*," we answered.

"Ah, you should know Bohemian"—and he expatiated on its beauties; "you should certainly stop awhile and learn it." And then he went on to state that the grammar would take us fifty years.

On another point we received enlightenment. "Are there any mathematicians in England?" he enquired.

"A few—perhaps at Cambridge," said the Observer modestly.

"Ah, but it is a great study in Bohemia. We possess the finest mathematicians."

From my humble acquaintance with the craft, I should be inclined to hail with joy the introduction of a Bohemian mathematician.

Next day, after shady by-roads along the sides of fields, where oxen ploughed long furrows, another schoolmaster spoke to us under the trees of Černoušek, enjoying himself during the vacation in shirt-sleeves and a white waistcoat. And at Ctiněves, a tiny hamlet, we had actually to use Bohemian words. We left our machines there, and ascended the Georgsberg, concisely styled Řip in the native tongue.

Řip was our first encounter with the volcanic cones that form such bold features in the northwest of Bohemia. They are recent enough to be well preserved, and were associated, indeed, with the later earth-movements of Europe. The country became "starred" and cracked between the Karpathians and the Erzgebirge; volcano after volcano rose upon the plateau of older rocks; and, though the sea flowed for a long while in the neighbourhood of Vienna, the dry land was here emerging and folding itself towards its present contour. These slow and titanic struggles, with their fierce little cracklings all along the line, left important traces in Bohemia. Not only have we the scattered cones and craters and sheer-sided volcanic necks, but the last phase of activity is still with us in the mineral springs along the frontier.

From the basalt cone of Řip we enjoyed a glorious view over the Elbe, with Maria Theresa's fortress in the foreground, and the German lands beyond. In the north-east a pleasing group of volcanoes, with one bold castle in the midst, went far to remind one of Auvergne. The whole floor of the country lay as if burnished in the sunlight; here and there a few black lines of poplars marked the main roads among the narrow close-set fields, which stretched up the slopes in every tint of brown and gold. On the summits, which looked almost level from our view-point, patches of dark woodland still remained. Far in the north the old granite barrier of the Erzgebirge lay like a blue wall, uniform and shadowless in the haze. Behind us the smoke of industry made one or two dusky little clouds on the horizon.

"There is Prag," said an officer, who had climbed with us to the chapel.

At Roudnice (Raudnitz) we again ferried the Elbe, and tried to swim in the wide shallow water, which was almost as warm as the pebbles on the bank. The merry little boys of Roudnice wade across from shore to shore, clamber on to the timber-rafts that come down swiftly with the current, and then drop off them on the other side. A few ships high and dry, and multitudes of expiring molluscs, showed that a hot season was upon us.

We now found ourselves in a German area, amid unfenced hop-gardens and feeble roads, made of pebbles lightly heaped together. The sunset behind the tumbled volcanic masses west of us was enough, however, to atone for human imperfections. This was a fête-day, and the great inn of Liebeschitz, mysteriously styled *Zur goldenen Sechs*, was crowded with young men and maidens, the latter coming in bareheaded, their coloured kerchiefs thrown around their necks, every one very bright, and as beautiful as circumstances would allow. Circumstances, let us admit, were not unkindly.

Our next few days were spent in climbing

up and down among charming woodlands on the fringes of volcanic cones, such as the huge Geltschberg, with its white phonolites, and the vale of Algersdorf, with its grand dark andesites and basalts. The phonolites are a feature of this area, and form, by their viscid coherent nature, extraordinary domes of rock. They

At Algersdorf

welled up in the necks of the volcanoes, or even flowed out in pudding-like masses, resembling the Grand Sarcouy of Auvergne. The weather attacks them round about, and they stand up as singular sheer-sided bluffs, perhaps a thousand feet above the lower hills. The rock itself is, in typical forms, a beautiful one—a soft compact grey-green, weathering to brown, with a delicate glassy lustre when freshly broken. The name is a mere translation, for international usage, of the old German *Klingstein*, referring to the note given out when the fissile slabs are struck. Those who are not geologists will yet rejoice with us when we say that the Wolf Rock, off the coast of Cornwall, an almost inaccessible islet, is the only spot where phonolite occurs unaltered in the British Isles. Imagine, then, the joy of riding in Bohemia from one crag to another, smiting the solid masses with the hammer, and seeing the lustrous flinty chips go skimming across the sunburnt grass.

The marvellous and fantastic country of the Hegau, between Constanz and Schaffhausen, shows one similar features; and the fortresses of the Hohentwiel and Hohenkrähen are built upon crags of phonolite. The lords of this earth have always found safety in volcanoes—at any rate, like Spartacus, in dormant ones.

We visited the busy valley of the Polzen, where the houses are built of brown timbers stopped with white along the horizontal lines, a pretty novelty in chàlet-work. The rich woods of the frontier have prevented the introduction of the stucco-renaissance of the south. The towns are pure straight-lined German, clean and neatly painted, with here and there some red-roofed château as a memory of feudal days. At Tetschen an officer of the castle was being buried, and the procession coming down the hill, with its band and priests and ecclesiastical banners, was a sympathetic touch amid the chimneys of the factory-town.

The Elbe runs here between steep rocks and woods, with pine-rafts on it, and little ships, and bathing establishments, and all the appanage of the Rhine. We were surprised, however, after being so long accustomed to regard ourselves as Personages, not persons, to run one night into Gross Priesen, and to have to sleep out in a private house kindly found for us by the hotel-keeper. It is well to come down into the world again, even to a world of garden-seats and little café-tables; touring in Hungary is too princely.

The Elbe became in time expensive. At Gross Priesen it had grown wider, and the ferry cost four kreuzers; but the prospect was charming, the red-roofed villages nestling among the trees, and the girls standing in a row upon the bank to see us off. Then at Aussig (Usti of the southerners) we had a fine bridge, value six kreuzers; and it led us to the grand old fortress of the Schreckenstein, on a crag of roughly columnar phonolite, rising sheer from the water's edge. The castle itself is built partly on overhanging masses of the cliff. Somewhere hereabouts, Prokop, the tonsured general of the Hussites, smote the Saxons out of the country, and then went south, with cheerful fervour, and polished off Austria and Hungary.

While we sat in a little inn at the Schreckenstein, and quaffed our raspberry-lemonade, the air melted the cement from under our tyres, though we had sheltered the machines beneath the vine-trellis of the garden. When we started again, the cement oozed out in strings and ringlets in a most undignified manner. To this also we were to grow accustomed.

A sloping footpath led to the shore, and the young ferryman got us all aboard, and out again, up a perilous plank, at Wanow (quadruple fee, in recognition of bravery, 20 kr.) That night we pushed up a steep side-valley, and abode *zum goldenen Kreuz* at Welemin, with a gilt crucifix above the door, and the huge cone of the Mileschauer towering against the northern twilight.

Welemin must have been always pretty; but here again the accommodation for strangers was probably unsuited to the Sage of Chelsea. No doubt the village has grown neater since his critical eye fell on it; but it cannot have been entirely rebuilt. The "broken-backed sleepy-looking thatched houses, not in contact, and each as far as might be with its back turned on the other, and cloaked in its own litter and privacy"—was this all that the Sage could see in Welemin, perched in the passage of the hills? One fancies his notes must have got jumbled, until we come upon a vicious little thrust at the "Czech Populations," and then the matter is explained.

Frederick the Great—a title we leave him gladly, seeing how such things are attained—marched one day through Welemin, where he knew his way already, and slew three thousand Austrians and three thousand of his own men down across the woods at Lobositz. Whereon he piously wished "to Heaven that the valour of my army might procure us a stable peace." It was another Prussian who desired at Saarbrück in 1870 "to live in peace with the French people." The results of such good-will are generally the same in the long run.

We had great geologisings among the cones; up the Mileschauer, with half Bohemia in a dead hot haze below us; down to Schima, with the wall of Saxony looming vast above the tumbled foot-hills; and finally away among the latter, and through the dusk to Schönau, the handsome suburb of Teplitz. Daily at 8 a.m. it would be 30° C. (nearly 90° F.) in the shade; and we began to ride cautiously, and to spend the noonday among the woods, or at the back of some little inn, in the company of carts and fowls and children, writing out our notes, and waiting for the shadows to grow longer.

Day after day dawned cloudless; the wind was warm and parching, carrying with it fine alluvial dust; a week of such days made one realise the Sahara. Yet to those who love the sunlight, it was wholesome and satisfying to the soul, though the rocks became too hot to handle and the grass too slippery to climb. The sun rose out of the central cornland, and set in triumph beyond the hills; and the blue nights were clear and very full of stars.

The following notes will express the situation better than any thermometric record:—

19th August 1892.—*Articles consumed by M. or N. between* 12 *noon and* 7.30 *p.m.*

    1 *Eiscafé* (observe the local spelling).
    1 *Glas Wasser* therewith.
    1 *schwarzer Kaffee.*
    1 *Glas Wasser* therewith.
    1 *Eiscafé.*
    1 *Glas Wasser* therewith.
    1 *grosse Flasche Bilinwasser.*

2 *Tassen Thee.*
3 small rolls.
1 half-slice *Hausbrod.*

Cost of above:—Drinks, 110 kreuzer; foods, 8 kreuzer.

Verily, it is as gross as Falstaff; and the curious may remember that he, at any rate, set a whole capon against the sack.

The Bořen of Bilin

It is cheap to drink the waters in the volcanic zone, and they fall in price as you approach their fountain-head. The ubiquitous Giesshübler had dropped from 30 kr. to 18 kr. (3½d.) in Teplitz, and the double-size bottles of the saline Bilin, always cooling and delectable, sank to 10 kr. in the town itself. Cry of the cyclist, "*A Bilin!*"

The enormous boss of phonolite, the Bořen of Bilin, is only one of many in these singular landscapes. It is visible miles away across the cultivated uplands, sheer and startling, with the Schladnigberg and others at its side. A fine cone, in this case tree-covered, occurs at Brüx, where, for the chimneys and the smoke-blasts, we might as well be at home in the Black Country.

Schladnig and the Schladnigberg

The smoke of factories is assisted by the curious Brown Coal deposits about Dux. This is a light compact material, on the way to become coal, of Oligocene and Miocene age. It is largely excavated for household purposes, and in some of the wide open pits we saw flames leaping here and there, and smoke rising from every crevice like steam in the crater of a volcano.

"Why is this burning?" we asked an artisan in the road.

"No one knows," he answered, laughing.

"Is it the great heat?" asked the Observer.

This seemed considered as an excellent joke. We pushed our enquiries further.

"Does it burn of itself?"

"*Ja, natürlich!*"

"How long has it been going on, then?"

"Four—no, five years. It burnt those buildings over there."

And this continues day and night, killing off grass and trees, and spreading to mine-engines and cottages on both sides of the imperial highway. However, with the great human smoke-drift blowing up from Brüx, we presume it is held to matter little. On this head no Englishman can complain; we had more charming landscapes once from Dudley to Sheffield and the Tyne.

At Gross Priesen an old man had judged us by our costume to be Tyrolese; at Brüx the waiter courteously remarked, "Surely the gentlemen come from the East?" Haply we did; but our romance was running to its close.

It is a fine road up to Karlsbad, and one welcomes the first spurs of the mountains. Klösterle has piled itself on an uncomfortable slope, with a slanting paved market-place, and a fountain ringed about with nude mythological statues, quaint enough in such surroundings. Space is valuable, for the town has to avoid the gorges of the Eger.

Thereafter one is really on the flank of the Erzgebirge, where the pines again gather thickly on the rocks. At euphonious Damitz the road makes a still bolder excursion, as if to try its strength. The great sun struggles over into Saxony, and the sky-line grows black against a golden air. Still there is the warm smell of the fir-woods, far into the breathless night; and the streams, no longer dark and stagnant, plash round the boulders, tremulously leaving the cool granite hills. A bird sweeps across the valley; and there is a rustling of some animal, perhaps a lizard, in the brown fir-spines by the road. All the town-bands of Teplitz, as one drinks the waters in the Kurgarten, cannot make music such as this.

THE HEART OF EUROPE

We saw the river Maine fall into Rhine,
Whose banks are set with groves of fruitful vines.
        MARLOWE. *Faustus.*

THE Grand Dukes and Excellencies who frequent Karlsbad—Karlovy Vary, we yet may have to call it—should buy up some of the mines on the adjacent summits, and should decorate their works with *Sprudelstein* and fancy ornaments, and make their engines smoke-consuming, and replace the dusty traffic by trim electric traction. Then the country would be worthy of the great fancy-fair of Karlsbad.

The town, however, lies very prettily in a groove of the granite plateau, not in any way rivalling Matlock in its scenery, but far surpassing it as a town. The cyclist, again, has far the best of it in the picturesque run from Klösterle to Schlackenwerth. But, after all, the waters are at Karlsbad.

In the well-kept narrow streets, under formal

classic colonnades, spring after spring gushes up, kept in hand and domesticated by pipes and little basins. Every one walks about with a cup slung on a strap across the shoulder, like a field-glass on an English race-course; and at your favourite spring, under strict medical advice, you drink without charge and without danger. Any way, these waters are warranted to be natural, and every geologist should taste them. It is really beautiful to watch the geyser of the Sprudel shooting up in hot splashes and steam into the air, and to feel in touch with the old volcanoes, even in a watery stage. The heat of it (162° F.) is still interesting enough. "Why go to the Yellowstone?" we again asked of one another.

We found our old friends, the gaberdined Jews of Galicia, walking about among the visitors of Karlsbad. But they looked forlorn and out of place. A Society for the Social Exhilaration of Polish Jews would meet with much sympathy, but probably with scant success.

The *Kaiserstrasse* still beckoned to us, leading away to the core of central Europe, the watershed of the Elbe and the Danube and the Rhine. The country was picturesque throughout, with incidents like the town of Elbogen, piled on the wooded bank of the Eger around a superb old Teutonic citadel.

Our last Bohemian night was spent up among the ridges of the fir-woods, in the *Goldener Spiegel*, a purely country inn. Herr A. Hofmann, the young proprietor, had spent eleven seasons in a hotel in Karlsbad, and so discharged on us a few words of English, which sounded very oddly in the highlands. He has married and settled down here, a healthy peaceful life, with a fine wide landscape at his door, and a seat under a tree in front of it, from which he can watch the traffic of the German road. An odd little wooden hut, a field or two down the slope, covers what we have styled the *Spiegelbrunnen*, a healing water highly charged with iron and carbonic acid. It belongs to the Count of Falkenau, who does not trouble to exploit it. Here is a spot for any lover of the country-side, condemned otherwise to the *salons* and parades of Franzensbad. The host and hostess of the *Spiegel* are hereby "highly recommended," and the inn itself is charming in its simplicity.

A mile below, in the next hollow of the road, the Liebau Bach comes cold and clear out of the hills; and I went down and bathed in it at sunset. All was absolutely still; the grass was a gentle blue-green in the twilight, almost the colour of the pines; and, in a notch of the woodland, one could see the last sunset flooding all the valley of the Eger. There are times when the hum of business and the challenge of the cheery stockbroker seem so far away as to resemble some one else's dream.

We had a day round Eger, no longer a fortress of the frontier, but fine enough with its castle, and red roofs, and old Gothic houses, with tier on tier of little windows. Readers of Schiller will remember it; and one may still conceive the tumultuous apprehension of that night in February, when the news spread that the last Free-Captain had passed from the reckoning of Europe. It was fully time; he was born to be a prince of the Renaissance, an age when conscience waited on desire. In the last struggle there is something fateful—Wallenstein, with his arms stretched out, taking the halberd of Devereux in his breast. Plague on the Greek traditions, which held Schiller's hand and soul at such a moment!

From Eger we visited the fascinating scoria-cone of the Kammerbühl; the fields around are strewn with ashes; it is as if this petulant little volcano had just broken through the old rocks of the plateau, and had heaped up the fragments and the scoriæ on any bright Bohemian day. It is hard to believe that this incoherent little hill is older than all human history.

Goethe, who did most things, defended the Kammerbühl, supporting its claims as a volcano; and the essay may be found reprinted in his works, "*herausgegeben und eingeleitet von S. Kalischer, dreiunddreissigster Theil,*" page 341. The Kammerbühl is charming as a model, standing by itself among the cultivated lands; and the whole thing might have been the work of a few hours.

I was riding up the broad avenue of Franzensbad, when I met its only noonday occupant, the policeman, who informed me that cycling was forbidden. So we walked down again together; the guests were all at their siesta, and he was glad of somebody to talk to.

"Of course," I said, "machines might frighten the horses."

"No; it is because of the visitors—they would all be riding—hither and thither—uncontrollable—*ach*, it would be *schrecklich!*"

I wish we could give this gentle guardian a glimpse of western cycling—say, a day in Dublin, at the corner of College Green.

Thunder rolled, and great welcome rain-drops fell, as we left Eger for the frontier. The air at last was cool across the dripping fir-woods, and a superb copper-red sunset flared through the serrations of the trees. At the Austrian custom-house the official lead seal was cut from the Observer's bicycle; thenceforward we were exiled and disowned. Presently a train came past us out of Germany; we saluted it—and behold, by a little stream, the blue and white Bavarian posts. Down at Schirnding the larger inn rejected us, probably because we were Bohemians; but the *Hirsch*, always a gentle creature, took us in, though it was difficult to find places in the tiny *Gastzimmer* among the smokers and their thick brown beer. We thus slept again among the mountains, while unwonted mists crept, chill and ghostly, into all the hollows of the woods.

Thence we went uphill for twenty miles, climbing the broad back of the Fichtelgebirge in easy stretches, between white-barked birch-trees and mountain-ashes with orange and scarlet clusters; while on either side the rolling curves of gneiss and granite were cultivated as cornland to the very limits of the pines. The summit comes at Hölle, a village of the woodland, and for a few minutes we could look down into the Danube basin before descending to the Main. On our left lay Baireuth; and the magnificent road ceases to take interest in the traveller when he passes the turning for that sacred city. The highway, in fact, is practically abandoned—a thing not uncommon in these days of railways. Has not, for example, the Inverness coach-road been turned into a grazing ground on the summit of the Grampians? The hills were gruesome, and covered with wanton boulders; and we walked patiently up and down. In the midst of this scene of savagery came Wiersberg, still 1500 feet above the sea, a steep nook in the hillside, which tourists have deservedly discovered. We had to climb out of it again, after the manner of a Devonshire combe, and to walk down, clutching at the brakes, on Ludwig Schorgast. Blessed be Ludwig, for he preferred to be connected with the world, even at the risk of waking some morning to find cannon pulled up at his front door. A good road soon developed; the final ten miles went within the hour; and we came in the dusk to Burgkundstadt, a richly quaint old town.

The houses are built in tiers on and against a sandstone cliff, connected by steep passages and flights of steps; and part of the upper town is supported on a castle-platform, buttressed out towards the valley. The beautiful lines of the timber-work are here whitewashed over; but most of the villages on the Main show a wealth of brown or black carved woodwork, with elaborate dormers, and fine clusterings of red roofs. To any west-country Englishman these are very welcome sights.

The weather had turned, and a cool wind blew against us from the ridges; it seemed already the breath of the Atlantic seaboard. We went one day up to Coburg to fetch our letters—a self-centred, self-sufficient little place, with a huge château on the hill-top, and comfortable villas in the valley. There is a feudal gateway; also a typical old market-place, with a characterless statue of Prince Albert in the centre of it. Coburg is an epitome of German ducalism; there is just enough antiquity about it to prevent it seeming wholly artificial.

We found our way out again into Bavaria, and slept in a rural wilderness, where half-timber hamlets lie lost in the clearings of the forest. You struggle along the sandy and stony ways, and suddenly come upon a group of cottages and a grey church-spire. Surely they must have grown there, moulded by their environment, like the ragged wind-caught pines. At Ober Elldorf the inn was signless; but such sweetly primitive places are the true guest-houses. You will find no advertisement of them, even in those two hundred pages of *Bradshaw's Continental Guide*. The tariff, however, deserves mention:—two meals and a bed, two shillings.

Königshofen, on the glorious *Königsstrasse*, is a gem of German picturesqueness. One could

want no finer contrast than these familiar steeply-pitched red roofs, these small shuttered windows, these church-towers bevelled off at the angles, terraced, bulbous, and spinose all at once, and the broad and joyous parody of Palladio that had beamed on us at Německý Brod. The fifteenth meridian is like "the Line" of old sea-voyagers. On one side are the traditions of London, Paris, or Berlin; beyond it lies an enchanted world.

At Saal we met the first beggar we had seen since Hungary—and there they were only gypsies. Our English roads are not so fortunate; I remember one summer day from Lancaster to Warrington counting four to every mile; and there is not much hesitation about your "tramping" western borderer.

With great public spirit the *Königsstrasse* has been carried out of the valley, over a huge hill, and steeply down on Neustadt, to show all the glories of the earth, and particularly of the Rhöngebirge, which we had to cross ere nightfall. This was the first of three forest-ridges that lay between us and the Rhine, each of them capped with volcanic débris exploded through the floor of Europe. We pushed up from Bischofsheim, in the cool delightful woods, until the road succumbed and gave place to grass and stones. And so we walked over into Hesse, and descended on the vale of Gersfeld, with the lights of little mountain-farms on the great grey slopes around us.

THE LAST DIVIDE

The goat is a clambering creature, that delights in climbing up rocks and precipices; and in the same manner the matters destined to this lower globe strongly affect to rise upwards.

BACON. *On Pan.*

WE were out of Bavaria, at any rate; but here my knowledge of political geography fails me. Let us say that we proceeded across Germany—the precise limits of Hesse-Darmstadt, Nassau, and Prussia are suited only for competitive examinations. We shortly entered Fulda, where we found ourselves under the protection of St. Boniface, whose statue adorns the cathedral-square. His bones lie somewhere under the white Renaissance dome, remembered here, if forgotten among Englishmen. Yet he was born at Crediton about 680, and was educated at Exoncastre or Exeter—so the *Lives of the Saints* inform us. And this Winfrith, Bishop Boniface, proved himself a true apostle, full of an adventurous zeal and modesty, encouraging "pious men and virgins to come out from

England," and so to make a clearing in the heathen woods. Who can say what these fearless men of Devon, and these Wessex maidens, firm of heart and limb, did for the wild Frisian lands? We are apt to honour Drake and Hawkins, and the harriers of the Spanish Main; let us at least keep Winfrith's memory green.

Lauterbach

Ninth-century churches are not often to be seen—except perhaps in Ireland; but there is a charming little building in Fulda, St. Michael's, near to the cathedral, simplest Romanesque in style, and now efficiently restored; it possesses, moreover, a real round tower, surmounted by a tall conical roof.

Lauterbach, away to westward, is one of the

most pictorial of towns; we slept there in the castle, in which the landlord of the *Anker* Inn now holds his baronial court. Almost every house is red-roofed, with black timbers and whitewashed walls; and the buildings are crowded together in continual variety of form, with narrow passages between them into which the drainage flows. Nothing but a fire could improve the sanitation of such a place—a fact that struck us the more when cholera was closing round us. It is time that Lauterbach was gently depopulated and preserved as a national museum.

The Rhön had thus been traversed, and lay in long blue waves behind us. From Lauterbach we attacked the Vogelsberg against a good west gale, but with a perfectly-rolled basalt road to struggle on. The chief object from our window at Gersfeld had been a neat little cone catching the earliest sunlight; and the Vogelsberg, on the axis between the Main and Lahn, is a more extensively volcanic area—too uniform, in fact, and unbroken by special dykes or necks. A marvellous quarry in columnar basalt occurs close to Lauterbach on the ascent; the columns are exported in convenient lengths for gateposts or for the sides of roads, and some of them can be extracted twenty-one feet long and only nine inches in diameter.

The sudden fall of the ground from the divide gave us a grand tumbled view over the Devonian hills of western Hesse. Close at hand, high upon the great slope of the country, rose the basalt crag of Ulrichstein, crowned by a ruined tower.

At Lutter Hesse

The peasants of this quiet area are disguised as ancient schoolboys, in peaked caps, short blue Eton jackets, and dark waistcoats and trousers. Most of them are clean-shaven, except for whiskers, and present an aspect of absolute benignity, which I am sure does not belie their character. Among them the Jews stand out sharply, somewhat gloomily, with darker hair, beards, and usually a preference for round-topped hats.

For fatherly gentleness and consideration, commend me to these good old men of Hesse; and when, strictly by their medical advice, I took a glass of *Schnapps* with them in the little inn of Hörgenau, my union with this simple country life appeared complete.

We came down among the basalts, and through lovely little woods, to Grünberg; and thus to the valley of the sluggish Lahn, with the dull old towns of Giessen and Wetzlar on its banks. In the latter place the name of the *Hôtel Kaltwasser* was surely meant to attract cyclists. Goethe has dealt with Wetzlar, and we are now on too familiar ground.

But above us lay a third ridge of the old central European forest, the Westerwald, and the Observer promptly led the way towards it. Volcanic areas, fascinatingly spotted with red upon all geological maps, exercise an irresistible attraction.

It was a grand sunny morning as we ran up the valley of the Dill; yet at Werdorf a tragedy filled all the air with gloom. We were examining certain shales and andesites with the true abstraction of the scientist; when, lo! a careless wind blew, and started my tricycle on an evil course. I saw it move; I fled towards it; a small boy gazed with mingled terror and delight; an innkeeper, attracted by the frenzied cries of the cyclist, bounded from his doorway across the road. But it was too late; the dizzy bank was neared, and the machine sped over it, revolving twice in air. That somersault gave me the measure of its fall—"three mètres from the road," as I had to repeat afterwards to half the village.

The innkeeper and I descended the bank into a little strip of cabbage-field; never did cabbages appear so unattractive, so deficient in any sense of humour. The beauty of the scene was restored, however, when we saw that the steel of Humber had proved equal to the shock. The axle was bent in two places, three spokes were broken, and the wheels were naturally a little out of truth. I restored them to their normal form, found that the machine was wheelable, and sought the village-smith of Werdorf.

There is something consoling, and even cheerful, in doing one's best with the simplest means; and here was a real adventure of the road. Herr Schopp, the smith, was a young man, assisted by a younger brother. He had never dealt with a ball-bearing before, but faced the matter like a man of science.

"You think you can straighten this axle?"

I said. "Of course I can easily take it by train to Wetzlar."

The young man smiled; he had been educated at the trade-school in the city.

"This man," said a bystander, "can do anything that can be done in Wetzlar."

I was reassured. We removed the wheels, took the four bearings to pieces, poured forth the grimy little balls like hail into a tray, and brought the ill-used axle free into our hands. The workshop being a shed open to the road, we were visited by small boys and a large number of more respectable citizens.

A man appeared, bringing a horse to be shod.

"I cannot do it now," said Schopp, "you see we are a *Velocipedenfabrik*."

The dignity of Werdorf as an industrial centre had risen in the last half-hour.

The smith gently heated the axle and smote it into straightness. It was a delicate piece of work, the axle being tubular, and each half being constructed of four portions brazed together. But Schopp was proud of his hand and eye, and of the honour of the schools of Wetzlar. We were prouder still when we got the whole together again, screwed up the bearings, and found that the wheels spun gaily, and were good for another thousand miles.

During these two and a half hours, the Observer, whose patience is inexhaustible, had found a modest little inn, into which a "German band" soon entered, until the *Gastzimmer* became literally possessed by it. These wanderers played for their own pleasure over their beer, with terrific effect in the tiny room. As soon as they had gone, the burgomaster sent down the policeman in his brass helmet to fine the innkeeper for having music at unlawful hours. It would have seemed fairer to arrest the minstrels, but then there was only one policeman. Moreover, the honest innkeeper was always on the spot.

Later in the day, as we emerged from a bath amid the vegetation of the Dill, we met these musicians again, some of them well filled with liquor. Their leader, who was a great traveller, assured us that he preferred England to any country, notably to his own—it was so free— you could perform anywhere at any time. Alas! we knew it well in London.

That afternoon we rode into Sinn, where iron-works mollify the air. A little farther lies the ancient town of Herborn, where we found the German army in possession. But good Mr. Louis Lehr and his wife gave us their son's bedroom, though the house was full of soldiers; and from our balcony we had a fine view of the troops marching out into the Westerwald next morning.

The town is made of old timber houses fronted with scales of slate, with a quaint irregularity of eaves and gables; and the towered Rathhaus dominates it. At the end one has a glimpse of the winding Dill and a pleasant country of green fields.

For a sixth day the wind beat against us, as we rose over long rolls of wooded country to the summit of the Westerwald. The dark grey basalt road seemed as if smoothed with sandpaper; the air had become very cool and bracing; and the wide swelling forest, pine below and sunnier trees above, was a vast delight to see. Far to north and south it stretched, coating every hollow with dark green or distant grey, until it rose at last, fold on fold, in the highlands of eastern Nassau. Soldiers moved here and there across this large and airy landscape; and at the crest of one long hill, which we were fortunately riding, we came up suddenly between two lines of the Staff, the handsome old officers beaming on us from more or less tractable steeds. A charming night spent among them a year before, in the thick of the manœuvres of Alsace, had wiped away all our dread of these men of blood and iron.

Neither the admirable and accomplished Baedeker, nor the tourist of the Rhine, has yet touched the quiet hamlets of the Westerwald. At Salzburg—is there not another of the name?—we lunched in a tiny châlet entitled *Wirthschaft u. Krämerei*, some 1800 ft. above the sea. Milk is here the staple product, and there was much to remind us of the simple *burrons* of Auvergne. The castle and narrow street of Hachenburg brought us back to feudal Germany; along this route the houses have Herbornian fronts of slate, often grouped in patterns of stripes and arches and the ancient symmetry of suns.

Then the country becomes a table-land of corn and culture, and we are on the plateau of Devonian rocks, through which the Rhine has slowly carved its way. Here we found Dierdorf, another unknown townlet, where we were received in a hotel of the unpointed brick style of Silesia, called the *Nassauer Hof*, as a compliment to eastern travellers. We had crossed into the Prussian Rhine-Province a few minutes before, and now felt nearly home.

And so for the seventh day the west wind blew against us; for the seventh day we climbed into the woodlands, and pedalled down what ought to have been free descents. The deep side-valley of the Sayn, one of the characteristic gorges of the Rhineland, gave us a welcome shelter. Isenburg is squeezed into it, a village of fantastic wooden houses, with the Burg above, a majestic ruin among the vines.

At Bendorf we emerged into the great Rhinevale itself, and beheld the strip of busy towns

and the enthusiastic competition of tall chimneys. And then our goal lay before us, the towers rising in a broad and sunny haze; here were the gleaming reaches of the river, and the bridge, and the great fortress, a scene famous in the march of nations. Krakow to Coblenz, the Vistula to the Rhine—our pleasant passages were here complete.

Looking backward, as we sat in luxury *zum wilden Schwein*, prior to our railway-journey to Ostend, I found that this summer, out of thirty-eight sleeping-places, there were only nine of which I had previously known the names—which shows how edification may go hand in hand with pleasure. Yet who knoweth Turdossin and Zsarnócza, Béláház and Ričan; or who hath seen the vines of Melnik and the basalt heights of Ulrichstein? Some other travellers there were who knew them, and returned, and told the tale; but that was before the days of railways. The new knights-errant have a vast free world to conquer, patined richly with romance; and the threshold of it is very near us, at the Hook of Holland or Dieppe. But let him that rideth on a quest seek out a comrade from the Round Table which is in Camelot; for verily I believe the Observer to have been of that true company.

Homeward Bound

www.ingramcontent.com/pod-product-compliance
Lightning Source LLC
Chambersburg PA
CBHW032155160426
43197CB00008B/928